blue twilight

nature, creationism, and american religion

Langdon Gilkey

FORTRESS PRESS
MINNEAPOLIS

BLUE TWILIGHT
Nature, Creationism, and American Religion

Scripture is taken from the New King James Version, copyright
© 1979, 1980, 1982 Thomas Nelson, Inc. Used by permission.
All rights reserved.

Cover image: *A New Planet*, Konstantin F. Yuon, 1875–1958.
Tretyakov Gallery, Moscow. © SuperStock 2001. Used by per-
mission.
Cover and book design: Ann Delgehausen

Library of Congress Cataloging-in-Publication Data
Gilkey, Langdon Brown
    Blue twilight : nature, creationism, and American religion /
Langdon Gilkey
        p. cm.
    Includes bibliographical references and index.
    ISBN 0-8006-3294-X (alk. paper)
        1. Creation. 2. Creationism—United States. 3. Theology,
Doctrinal—United States. I. Title.

BT695 .G49 2001
231.7'65—dc21   2001018928

The paper used in this publication meets the minimum require-
ments of American National Standard for Information Sciences—
Permanence of Paper for Printed Library Materials, ANSI
Z329.48-1984.

Manufactured in the U.S.A.   AF 1-3294

05   04   03   02   01   1   2   3   4   5   6   7   8   9   10

blue twilight

this volume is dedicated to

Nathan Scott
Paul Goldstein
Ray Culver
Ali Jihad Racy
Sherwood Leighton
Bobby Rosenblum
Larry Latta
George Whitten
Indr Cheema
Roelof Oostingh
Rob Zwang
Arie Rijke
Jim Shields
Robert Denomé
E. J. Tarbox
Robert Pagani

contents

Preface   ix

Part 1: Light and Darkness in American Religion
1. The Theology of Nature   3
2. Human Nature and Myth in an Age of Science   11
3. The Creationist Controversy   21
4. The Religious Right   43
5. The Meaning and Relevance of Creation   55

Part 2: Theology's Struggle with Modernity
6. Reinhold Niebuhr   75
7. An Introduction to Tillich   87
8. Tillich and the Neoorthodox   99
9. American Theology since Niebuhr and Tillich   109

Part 3: Hopeful Illuminations
10. Plurality and Its Theological Implications   121
11. The Religious Situation
    at the Beginning of the New Millennium   143
12. History and Theology   157
13. Reflections on Mortality   169

Index   173

preface

Today elements of light struggle with darker elements in American religion and public life. In this volume, I trace this conflict to its sources in American Christianity's incomplete and unsuccessful addressing of questions posed by the modern world of science, technology, religious pluralism, and historical consciousness. I try to show what is at stake in this tumult, especially as we see it flare up in such battles as those over creation and creationism. I also gauge the work of two giants—Reinhold Niebuhr and Paul Tillich—for meeting those cultural challenges, and in the final chapters I look for redemptive light in our religious situation in a new millennium.

In reflecting on the religious issue or issues centrally operative in the larger historical events and movements of the second half of the twentieth century, my conviction is that history and the religious are deeply intertwined. As a consequence, historical reflection and theology are appropriately brought together in thinking about the causes and the consequences of events in time. Alike for good and for ill—and history shows it has been for both—ideology and something like religious faith appear and reappear in each age, secular or "religious." Hence the understanding of events, in our age as in the past, must include an understanding of the religious component of that age's life.

Five of these chapters (1, 6, 8, 9, and 11) originally
were written for delivery in Japan in the fall of 1999. The subjects of these addresses were assigned to me by my Japanese
hosts. Unfortunately, however, that trip had to be abandoned
at the last moment. When, therefore, my hosts in Japan later
asked for permission to publish translations of these addresses
in Japanese, it occurred to me to assemble them, along with
other recent efforts, into a volume for publication in the
United States. Hence the other essays in this volume were
added to this core.

Three themes dominate this volume. There is first of all
(part 1) the issue of religion and science. Prominent in that
matter is, of course, the question of creationism, or "creation
science," to which two chapters are devoted. Creationism represents the fundamentalist interpretation of the origins of the
universe and of life, a matter of the utmost political, scientific,
and educational as well as religious and theological significance. I was a witness against the creationists in the civil trial
in Little Rock in 1981, and for the decade and a half since, I
have spent a great deal of time addressing that subject in col-
leges, churches, and professional groups around the country.
Chapters 3 and 4 represent respectively an early and a recent
edition of those efforts (see my *Creationism on Trial: Evolution and God at Little Rock* [Minneapolis: Winston, 1985],
which has since been republished by the University Press of
Virginia [1998]). Other current aspects of the theme of religion
and science are the question of a theological understanding of
nature (chapter 1; for a fuller explication of this theme, see my
*Nature, Reality, and the Sacred: The Nexus of Science and
Religion*, Theology and the Sciences [Minneapolis: Fortress
Press, 1993])—a subject noticeably omitted in the first half of
the last century; the interesting and paradoxical question of
the interrelationship between nature and human nature
(chapter 2; an address given at the University of Oregon, May
2000); and finally, a nonfundamentalist interpretation (and,

so, not anti-scientific) of the meaning of the crucial Jewish and
Christian symbol of creation (chapter 5), an address that was
delivered at Loma Linda University in California in Septem-
ber 1999. (For a larger treatment of creation, see my *Maker of
Heaven and Earth: A Study of the Christian Doctrine of Creation* [Garden City, N.Y.: Doubleday, 1959].)

In part 2, I address the continuing relevance of Niebuhr
and Tillich, which represents the second general theme. Three
of the subjects (chapters 6, 8, and 9) were specifically re-
quested by my Japanese hosts, and, needless to say, they fitted
in very well with my own abiding interests (for example, see my
Gilkey on Tillich [New York: Crossroad, 1990], and *On
Niebuhr: A Theological Study* [Chicago: University of Chicago
Press, 2001]). The remaining one (chapter 7, "An Introduction
to Tillich") represented an address given in Highlands, North
Carolina, in June 2000, to the very lively theological and philosophical discussion group organized there by my friend of
many years E. J. Tarbox.

With the third theme we return to issues of systematic or
constructive theology. During the final three to four decades of
the twentieth century, a major theological question arose with
new force—as had concurrently the issue of nature. This was
the question of the plurality of religions, that is to say, how each
religion is to understand itself in the quite new situation of what
we may call a "recognized rough parity" with other religions.
(Let us note that this is not unlike the analogous question: how
is a culture—say, Western culture—to understand itself in the
light of a newly recognized "parity" of cultures?) The question
of the parity of religions raises even more intense issues within
the theology of each religion than it does in the relations of that
religion to others, a relation now (on the whole) fortunately one
of mutual tolerance, increasing understanding, and growing dialogue. I have discussed this issue continuously in teaching, beginning with courses taught with David Tracy at Chicago in the
1980s, and continuing with courses on plurality at Georgetown

in the 1990s. The essay here (chapter 10) on plurality is a rough summary of these reflections. Chapter 11, "The Religious Situation at the Beginning of the New Millennium," was an address given in New Harmony, Indiana, at the annual conference on Tillich's thought in June 1999, hosted by the North American Tillich Society.

Chapter 12, "History and Theology" (delivered at Union Theological Seminary in Richmond, Virginia, December 2000), seeks to show the centrality of the "religious" component in an understanding of the present historical situation. (For a fuller explication of the theme of the intertwining of history and theology, see my *Reaping the Whirlwind: A Christian Interpretation of History* [New York: Seabury Press, 1976].) The volume concludes with a sermon on mortality—on the end, so to speak, of both history and theology—written for delivery in Japan in 1999.

The title of this book, *Blue Twilight*, has been inspired by the title to a favorite song of mine written and composed by my son, Amos Gilkey. The song "Blue Twilight" is one that appears on his superb compact disc titled *Drive*. I wish to thank Amos for allowing me to borrow this title.

This volume is dedicated with great affection and esteem to friends during these last years—some of them going back far too long to admit! And whatever light this volume may contain is surely owed to the love and support of my family: Sonja, Amos, Frouwkje and Stephane, and Whitney, Laura, and Sofia.

Part 1
Light and Darkness in American Religion

1

the theology of nature

If I were asked what are the biggest changes in theology since the first half of the twentieth century, since the great neoorthodox days, I would mention, first, the concern for the issue of the pluralism of religions, and second, the deep, and very new, theological concern with nature. Nature was almost ignored in the biblical revival of the 1920s and 1930s. As Karl Barth said in 1918, nature is the backdrop for the human drama with God, the stage on which that drama is played out; otherwise it is of little theological interest. And his contemporaries agreed with him. All repeated the affirmation of God's creation of all things, but while each provided a careful theological (biblical) anthropology or view of human nature, none offered a thoroughly worked out theological account of nature.

There were several understandable reasons for thus overlooking nature, amazing as it is now to us, reasons both methodological and substantive. The most important, I believe, was (on the part of theologians and clerics) the awe at and fear of natural science and scientific technology, awe at a vast cultural force they did not understand, and fear that science, with its objectivist understanding, would overwhelm the human and the personal in theology if it were allowed in, so to speak. In that period, science was rapidly becoming dominant, not only in cultural but also in intellectual and academic life. And science then saw itself as a totally objective study of the objective world, the world of objects—the world of "its," to use Martin Buber's word—a world totally dominated by necessitating, or seemingly so, chains of causality.

Few in the wider culture disputed this picture of science as objective and realistic, or of nature—insofar as science could know it—as a determined realm of causes and effects. Only Whitehead among the philosophers challenged this view, and his influence in philosophy was fast disappearing. Perhaps to its own surprise, theology thus appeared as the defender of the human, greatly helped by the existentialist revolt also against an objectifying science. With the help of the categories of Kierkegaard and Buber, theology thus emphasized the personal character both of the human and of God. For most biblical or neoorthodox theologians, science studied the world of I–it, the world of nature, while true theology and philosophy explored the quite different world of I–thou, though, as with the Romantics, whom these theologians also resembled, nature could under certain special human conditions become a "thou."

Second, theology in the first half of the twentieth century was concerned almost exclusively with *history*, the realm of the human, of freedom, and of novelty, which it sharply distinguished from nature, the realm of necessity and recurrence. This, too, is not surprising. It was history that was terrifying the theologians. These were the decades (from 1915 to 1945) when culture and history seemed suddenly to become suffused with violence, cruelty, and oppression. Seemingly civilized nations erupted into barbarism, invading their neighbors and oppressing them. In short, history appeared to become demonic, ruled by overwhelming malevolent forces. Hence the myth of historical progress, which the entire West and the new East had believed in, vanished after 1918 in Europe and after 1934–40 in America. It vanished like a happy dream, and the world awoke to the nightmare of conflict, tragedy, and suffering, and of the reality of sin as their major cause. History is never comfortable, though the nineteenth and early twentieth centuries thought it now well under control. But it can become quite out of human control, dominated by irrationality and evil, as it seemed to be in the second, third, and fourth decades of the twentieth century. No wonder theology concentrated, not on evolutionary development (it ignored this!) but on historical crises: catastrophe, suffering, sin, and guilt.

Nature in Crisis

We live in a quite different historical epoch, and it is wise—in fact, honest—to recognize these cultural influences on theology. We have discovered, roughly since 1965–70, that human industrial and technological development, and back of that science, endanger not just the human world but even more the natural world, on which human civilization is utterly dependent. This is a terrifying thought that was, I believe, quite inconceivable in the first two-thirds of the twentieth century. Like its biblical and prophetic predecessors, theology must be awake to events in its historical world. And perhaps the major event in our present world is the endangering of nature—of air, water, earth—and therefore the threat to the possibility of life itself. It is the sudden awareness of the ecological crisis, arising only, say, in 1969, that understandably has created the new intense interest in a theology of nature.

We should note, however, that although this is a crisis for nature—in which an endangered nature becomes an object of great concern—it is not a crisis brought on by the forces of nature. On the contrary, it is a crisis brought on by humans, that is, by the infinite human scientific, technological, and industrial creativity on the one hand combined with the insatiable greed or concupiscence of humans (what Buddhists term *desire*) on the other. Desire, said Nishitani Keiji, not rational choice, runs our common industrial empire, and it is desire that threatens our earth. Hence the cause of the crisis of nature is *historical*, the devastation, familiar enough to history, that sin or *desire* makes to our common life. The crisis thus interestingly discloses that in our age, when rightly we concentrate on nature, actually it is *history* that has finally triumphed over nature; history, corporate human action, can and does endanger nature, though as this crisis *to* our existence also discloses, history remains utterly dependent upon nature. This is the paradoxical irony of our situation: we arise from nature, but such is our creative power that we can also destroy her and, in destroying her, destroy ourselves.

Concurrent with the ecological crisis, a new understanding of science has arisen that promises to make science much less directly antithetical to theological and philosophical reflection. This has been labeled the "New Philosophy of Science"; clearly it is a reflective response to the new physics of probability and even of indeterminism. The assumed objective and universal causal determinism of another era has vanished, remaining for some but only as an article of faith. In its place has come an uncertainty about how to speak of what we know in our formulae, and a sense of the deeper mystery of the reality of the nature we seek to know. Correspondingly, attention in the philosophy of science has focused on the subject, the inquirer, as partly determinative of scientific knowing—what she brings to the inquiry in metaphysical assumptions, in paradigms and models, and in commitments to the scientific community and its norms. In other words, science here is seen as *perspectival*, relative to its historical and cultural time and place, a *hermeneutical* search for structures of meaning in experience rather than a direct look at reality as it is. As is evident, it is much easier to relate such an inquiry, so understood—with its assumptions, its models, and its commitments—to philosophy and theology, these latter being a reflection on the assumptions necessary for scientific inquiry, than it was a generation or so ago.

Finally, as a result of this new theological concern for nature and this new rapprochement between theology and natural science, a new sort of theological writing has developed in the last half century. These genres, to be sure, have always been present; nonetheless, they were given little notice during the neoorthodox days. A great deal of excellent literature has appeared—by both scientists and theologians—on the relations of science and theology, represented notably by Arthur Peacocke, John Polkinghorne, and Robert Russell, all scientists concerned with theology. They have produced evident and interesting natural theologies, as has, of course, Paul Davies. And among those involved in theological construction, one finds a much more substantial influence of evolutionary thinking, whether in studies of nature, in theological anthropology, and especially in the doctrine of God, represented by such names as Gordon Kaufman and Philip Hefner, and in a less important mode, my own recent work. Much of science, reflected and unreflected, remains within the earlier paradigm of an objective study of the determined sequences of natural causality, but insofar as there is this new understanding of science, there is much more room for interchange today than ever before.

A Theological Response

Our next important question concerns the relevance of this matter to theology. The crisis, we said, is a crisis for nature, but it remains a crisis in history, a crisis brought on, as are all historical crises, by the destructive possibilities of corporate human action. The crisis, therefore, illustrates, as does all of history, the universality as well as the reality of human sin. Moreover, as in all cases of social human sin, it is the ruling, dominant, and thus wealthy groups that are most visibly responsible and so guilty. If, as I am suggesting, the crisis is at base one of the spirit, then clearly the partial resolution—and that is all we can hope for in history—must also be one of the spirit, in the end a moral and a religious resolution.

Of course, this is a crisis in which initially science takes the leading role. It is science that has warned us of the impending dangers to nature, and it continues to do so; and it is scientific knowledge and wisdom that must direct the healing process. But since this process also involves powerful economic and social forces, the resolution is as well—and perhaps primarily—a political problem. Corporate responsibility and self-control—for example, the stemming of the heedless industrial and real estate development—can only be achieved politically through vast and concerted government action. Such common political and social action in turn requires intellectual and moral assent on the part of significant populations. It requires a new sense of common human responsibility for nature, for nature's preservation, and so, inevitably, a new respect for nature's integrity. As every intelligible political ethic affirms, and especially Christian social ethics, power involves responsibility else it be totally destructive. We humans now have an almost infinite power over nature, over her life and death. This power, therefore, forces us to treat nature responsibly: with justice, with care, and with respect—a respect for nature's value for herself, value in herself and not just her value for us.

This should, needless to say, be an obvious Christian moral requirement, like the obligation to treat every human as an end in herself and not merely as a means. Yet, as we noted, it was never fully understood until only yesterday. Perhaps one of the reasons is that the Scriptures recognize only humans as made in the image of God, and that nature seemed to be there only, so to speak, for our prudent use. We should recall, however, that it took a very long time as well for us to recognize the inherent value of every human being, of whatever race, gender, nationality or religion—despite our Christian certainty that all were made in the divine image! Nonetheless, it has, I believe, been the Jewish and Christian belief that all humans are made in God's image which has, more than anything else, led to the gradual recognition that slavery, racial intolerance, gender abuse, and national and class prejudice are unacceptable because each person has a value for God and hence in herself. As God's creation, I am now suggesting, nature is also an image or a mirror of its divine Creator, and thus does nature have a value in itself.

That nature mirrors or images God is clearly stated in many psalms and certainly in Job (Psalms 8, 19, 29, 50, 65, 77, 95–98, 103–4, 121, 136, 147–48; Job 9, 12, 28, 38–39): it is in and through the forces of nature that the glory, power, and wisdom of God are shown to us. The most fundamental attributes of the biblical and Christian God are precisely these: infinity, power, life, and order or wisdom. These represent the "glory" of God and form the conceptual base for the biblical and Christian idea of God. We may well ask ourselves how these concepts have arisen in our consciousness, where in Hebraic and in our own experience these categories are known and then applied as symbols to God. For certainly God's power, life, and order are as unlike our own as much as they are like our own. The only aspect of our experience in which immense and unlimited power, life, and order are known to us is in our experience of nature—more surely for the Hebrew than for us, encased as we are in a humanly crafted environment. It is through nature's power, order, and beauty that the divine power, order, and beauty have been manifested to us.

In short, I would suggest that the fundamental character of the God of Scripture—as infinite and eternal power, life, order, and wisdom—has been disclosed to us initially through the mirror of nature, as the infinite love and care of God have been disclosed to us and made conceivable initially through a mother's and a father's love, a neighbor's care, even a stranger's concern—though it is only in revelation that these divine attributes have become clear to us. As the other religions show to us so well, it is in our universal experience of nature that these symbols or analogies of God—infinite power, life, and order—have come to us. What is universal and, to us, ambiguous in other traditions has been clarified for us and for our tradition in revelation, in God's coming to Israel and then to all in the reality of the Christ. As Calvin said, God is to be known in the

glory of nature, but such is the dimness of our eyes that we do not
see this. But when we put on the spectacles of Scripture, this
knowledge becomes clear, definite, and certain. Thus this is not
natural theology, but it is the assertion, necessary for any theology, that God is disclosed through nature's glory. And that means
inescapably that nature is a mirror or image of her Creator and
Preserver—and so of value in herself—just as we are.

This is a disclosure of power, not of righteousness; of
order, not of love; of indifference to ranks and privileges, not of
mercy; and of life, death, and new life, not of eternal life. In
each case, what is known of God in the word completes and
goes beyond what is known in our experience of nature.
Nonetheless, what is known in nature is a presupposition of
what is known in the word, a presupposition of the message
central to our faith.

We have learned recently from evolutionary science that
our personness—our uniqueness, creativity, the possibility of
our sin, and so of our redemption, the *image of God* in each of
us—is itself the result in space and time of long developing
natural processes. God has worked *through* this whole, long,
cosmic story and through the evolution of life, of our genetic
background, and of our physiology, to create the divine image
in us. Hence, and here is the crucial point, the most "personal"
aspect of our existence, and so the possibility of our redemption, those aspects of ourselves that Judaism and Christianity
have emphasized, are themselves the results of nature's creative
processes, under the power, the urging, and the creative plan-
ning of God. Under the guidance of its divine creator, the image
of God in us is itself the result of *the image of God in nature*,
through which God has created us as we are. This message is
plain to us today, first in our developing history and nature that
science gives to us, in our understanding of the biblical word,
and most urgently in our new realization of the vulnerability of
nature to our heedless power. Our age is thus one in which
the defense of nature has taken its place alongside the older
defense of the human as our primary objectives.

2

human nature and myth
in an age of science

At the outset, let me explain how I am using the word *myth*, and something of the ragged history of this concept in modern life. I am not sure how much this introduction should be changed for postmodernism, except that almost certainly general statements such as these are politically incorrect. Be that as it may, however much myths may vary in cultural contexts, from the very beginning their role seems to have been to tell us who we are at the most fundamental level: what the relation of we humans is to the massive powers of reality that brought us into being, what therefore our capacities and obligations in this given situation are, and thus what our destiny may be—what reasons there are for our suffering, our evil, and our death, and what grounds for hope and rescue there are.

As is obvious, it is no wonder that myth and religion are so inextricably associated. The center of concern for myth and for religion, namely, the nature and destiny of human beings, is clearly the same. Therefore myth has frequently been said to be the appropriate language for religion, for in both we are dealing with the most fundamental understanding we have of ourselves and our powers, of what makes up human nature. Also myth is here not being defined as ipso facto untrue; if, in fact, each culture is based on its own myth, then myth helps define truth for that culture. Let us also note that myth is not just about ourselves, our inner dilemmas, and our dreams. As every example of important myth, ancient or modern, shows, myths are also about the entire objective structure of reality in which we exist. Myth, therefore, is not primarily or exclusively psychological, nor is it to be interpreted that way.

Mythical language thus includes and grounds ontological and philosophical language, theological and ethical language, as well as scientific, psychological, social, and political discourse—and has spawned all of these out of its generous womb. Myth, in other words, relates outer and inner: who we humans are as subjects (as well as objects) in relation to our wider environment. Since we are in fact subjects and not robots, such a relation conceived inwardly is utterly necessary if we are to function as humans—as self-directive—in our families, our work, our knowing, our society, our fears, and our prospects. The myths of other peoples, especially of past peoples, are, of course, merely quaint to us: charming, of psychological import only, and a bit silly. Since we see everything *through* our myths when we look around us, we do not think we have myths. What we see is the real world and our own normal selves within it. It takes a bit of self-consciousness to realize that we, too, live in myths.

The Changing Role of Myth

When the modern period developed with the rise of science, the role of myth and of its language changed. Gradually the formation and shaping of common life by religious tradition diminished. Ordinary communal relations—social, economic, political—were given what we term "secular" bases. In turn, external reality was now defined largely by the new sciences as material, universally determined, and inwardly vacant, as Whitehead put it. The radical split between subjects with intelligence, purposes, and values on the one hand, and determined objects on the other, began. In such a dualistic world, there was no longer any room for myth: myths became on the one hand psychological fantasies, and on the other, untrue statements about outer reality. It may be said that one of the essential characteristics of modern culture was the conviction that it neither needed nor had any myths. Myths lay behind us in the now receding religious past of a developing race. But we have moved into the age of science; we now know how to know, and so we have no use for myths.

In a sense, of course, modernity was right regarding its own uniqueness. Before this age, most—though not all—myths were "nature" myths, grounded, as nature then appeared to be, in a cyclical understanding of time. Hence they were myths about origins, about the beginning, when the sacred powers-that-be established the permanent and universal natural structures of our experience. Modernity, however, not only discovered science and the scientific method of understanding, but it also uncovered—or uncovered in a new way—a new sense of human creativity and freedom, the golden gift of autonomy. As never before, it was seen that human creativity could effect changes in historical time in the character of civilization. This new realization about human creativity and historical change had many causes, but prominent among them, I believe, was the wonder of the new science. It was the appearance of a quite new mode of understanding, and with it a new world, I think, that made the second half of the eighteenth century newly conscious of change in historical time, of the appearance of the radically new in historical development, and of the apparent progress involved in that process. Hence, to the second half of the eighteenth and to the nineteenth century, history represented the gradual, scientific, technological, and democratic development of civilization. Let us note that this sense of change and development in history preceded by almost a full century the same sense of change and development in nature. We should note also the background in Hebrew and Christian eschatology of this sense of developing time. Progress and the material dialectic were the secular descendants of these biblical motifs.

In any case, our point is that concurrent with the disappearance of older myths of nature and of traditional religious myths of history, there arose in modern culture a new consciousness of the progressive development of history and of the bright prospects for the future in higher and higher civilization, *their* civilization—in short, a new myth. Origins ceased to represent the sacred seat of realized value as they did before; we moderns have not looked, as did the Chinese, to any earliest ancestors as role models. Now the locus of realized value was moved from the beginning into the future, in the age to come. Utopias in the age to come became the place where the final union of reality and the good would occur. Scornful of nature myths, the modern consciousness lived until only yesterday in the aura of its own new myths of a progressive history. The myth of progress characteristic of the democratic, capitalist world, still to be found alive and well among many in the sciences and social sciences, and the myth of the material dialectic together energized, shaped, and directed our common modern world.

Creature and Spirit

How are we to understand ourselves? If we are subjects as well as objects, spirit or mind as well as organic bodies (or spirit emerging from organic body), then we must understand ourselves as both flesh *and* spirit, as, therefore, related intrinsically to the whole of reality and not just to our immediate physical environment, crucial as that is. It has been the character of humanity since it appeared to understand itself as part of the whole to see itself in relation to what it took to be the sacred powers of things, and to view its life, its obligations, its norms, and its values in those terms. Thus humanity has understood itself and its world by means of myths—narratives that related its life to the sacred and the ultimately real. And, as I have tried to show, this has been the character of modern and postmodern women and men as it has been of our ancestors. We have viewed history, and ourselves in history, mythically, as undergoing a quite triumphant but dubious progress into rationality.

Let us dwell on these issues a little further. Our creatureliness is too evident in all of us to miss, perhaps especially when we get a bit older. But at every stage, we are physically radically dependent on air, water, food, moderate comfort, and so on—and on health, on the order and harmony of our organic being. And spiritually, we are also dependent on one another, in our sexuality, in families, in community. We know well that we need not be, that we can quickly cease to be; in short, we know that each of us is contingent, dependent, and mortal, that we all die. We are animals among other animals, and science can and does tell us more and more about what this means: from genetics, through biology and physiology, to physical anthropology and psychology. But remember: although the sciences of physics, genetics, chemistry, and behavioral psychology know objects and ourselves as objects, each science *as inquiry* demands mind or spirit as its own essential ground; it takes an intelligent, purposeful subject to do science. Science's method is based on requirements of logic, not on streams of causation. To know the genetic causes of genetics is not yet to understand the meaning or the validity of genetics; meaning and validity represent logical, not causal, relations. To know the causes of science or of religion is not the same as knowing its meaning and truth. The aim of science is truth. A passionate attachment to truth, a capacity of spirit, is one of the necessities if there is to be science. Finally, another prerequisite of science is moral integrity, the refusal to cheat even for salary or fame.

Without these "spiritual" bases, science withers and dies. Ironically, therefore, science represents perhaps the greatest *spiritual* achievement evident in modern civilization; we all wish that the moral and religious life of that civilization were equal in power! Thus it is unreflective, if not silly, for scientists, as some do, to insist that because they know only the objective, the determined, and the material (whatever that may mean in contemporary science!), and because science is for them the only way to know, therefore the objective world of matter in motion is all there is. They themselves are as inquirers the living proof of the reality of the subject, of spirit.

Granted this, it follows that we must understand ourselves as beings with spirit, as inner selves or persons, as well as objective bodies. And it also follows that just as a culture needs science to understand itself and its world, so it needs the humanities to comprehend at all what it is for us to be in that world. We represent a paradoxical, mysterious unity of the two, of creature and of spirit, of contingent, living mortality with a self-transcending spirit that reaches for infinity. This is a unity that, I suspect, cannot be easily understood from either side, that of science or that of the humanities. This unity transcends our easy modes of intelligibility, but we know from the inside as well as the outside that the unity is there.

We must eat, we suffer, and we die—and we know all this. We humans know we are mortal; we know we may be hungry next week or next year; we know we are threatened by others far out of sight, smell, or hearing—even across the globe. We therefore have the dynamic creativity of the human and the dynamic character of history, but also our deep anxiety and our resulting inordinate self-concern. Not only do we share the animal will to live, but we generate out of that animal will the human will to power. Thus we attack the neighbor who threatens us—physically, socially, spiritually, and (the last is the worst!) with a cruelty and a ruthlessness unknown in the rest of nature. We keep going even when we are full, and we pursue another enemy across another hill. And as moral spirits, in doing this we must tell ourselves that it is for the good (their good!), for God, for order and peace—even for justice! Humans are not only those who alone know that they die, but also the only ones who tell themselves that they kill others for the highest values. As Reinhold Niebuhr said, hypocrisy is the bow that sin makes to virtue.

Human Self-Understanding as Myth

I have mentioned all this to emphasize how paradoxical and strange we humans are and how complicated any sort of human self-understanding must be. Our self-understanding can be expressed only in terms of myth, a myth that includes the creatureliness with the infinity of spirit, the longing for the good with the immense capacity for evil—and with all of this, the possibility of growth, of inner transformation, of some measure of redemption. We long for love and for immortality, and yet all of us (for there are no simply "good guys") are capable of intense evil. No wonder that from the earliest times in each age, we have sought mythical language to describe ourselves and our destiny, from the simplest myths of origins in nature all the way to the modern myth of progress, of socialist dialectic, of the new age of scientific rationality and democracy. And each day the news reveals the other side, then and now: the self-love, the ambiguity, and the destruction that are also ours. Certainly science has no wish to understand this deep complexity *scientifically*, though many scientists are very wise here. And certainly a fundamentalist religion that thinks it is science and can replace science will never illuminate the paradoxical puzzle that is ourselves.

For this, we need to open ourselves again to symbolic and analogical speech, to mythical speech. We need to discourse at once about the foreground that science and social science uncover, and the heights and depths of creaturely spirit that the humanities can explore. We need to remember that each myth, being the self-understanding of a given, particular cultural community, reflects not only the immense creativity of that community's life but also its forms of sin: its racial, national, class, and gender prejudices. For myths are as dangerous as they are necessary; they are also engines of dominance and oppression. Thus, on the one hand, the symbols and analogies by which we understand ourselves and our world—the machine, the computer, our normal family values, democracy, security, peace—remain absolutely essential to our common life. On the other hand, each symbol and its use is *freighted*, as we believe it and enact it, with our partialities and our interests. We need, therefore, not only myths—the symbols and analogies dear to us—but *criticism* of our myths, the consciousness or awareness of our own ambiguity and self-concern, even about our highest values. We, even we, are relative, and all we hold dear is relative—would that Washington, Wall Street, Main Street, *and* academia understood that!

But not *all* can be relative. We cannot hold onto our values if all slides into relativity, the relativity of self-concern. The end of that road is cynicism, which merely continues the destruction. There is, however, an ultimate and an unconditioned that does not perish. That ultimate and unconditioned is the confidence that religious faith gives, as long as a part of that faith is the awareness of our own partiality and the judgment that we, too, even *in* that faith, are involved in the relativity. Thus mythical discourse moves, if it will complete itself, into the religious. And religion, if its issue it not to be destruction, must relate ourselves to something beyond us—beyond our partiality and relativity to something that judges us as well as supports us, and therefore something that can give us hope.

Our values, as we have said, are *our* values, expressed in terms of our common life, manifesting the unique character of our life. We who think about values see them rightly as *ours*, that is, as human, and so as projections from our social context and our psyches. Because of science, we know that nature—its history and processes alike—must be understood "objectively," unmixed as far as possible with our inner needs and fantasies. Hence we are tempted in an age of science to speak of our values and our norms essential to our common life as separate from and unrelated to our objective world, as science is to be separated from our ideological passions.

This familiar division between inward human values and objective world is thus at one level quite essential. And in our ordinary thinking, most of us live quite happily in this common dualism: a social and psychological inner existence in an objective, semidetermined world, the humanistic humanities on the one hand and the objective sciences and social sciences on the other. Such is therefore also the main structure of the university, and the essential philosophical (if we can call it that) grounding of its faculties. But as reflection has shown, this unreflected dualism makes little sense in actual experience. In ourselves and in our common life, objective and subjective, outer and inner, flesh and spirit, unite and act together in each moment and in each of our actions. In the most mysterious but common, everyday way, we are *one*. And as our human spirits are saturated with our creaturely relativity, so is our creatureliness saturated with spirit and mind. We are creatures who inescapably ask questions, not only about our bodies and not only about our inner life, but also about how we and our community should *be* and should *act*; and so we ask also about our world, our history, and our destiny—in short, about the whole. Our values necessary for inner and outer life must therefore be lodged firmly in this entire reality, from which and in which we exist, if they are to be valid. We exist not only within our own nature, inner and outer, and not only in the immediate world around us, but also in the heights and depths of the Ultimate Being or whole that grounds us and supports us. Our self-understanding must be mythical and transcendent as well as scientific and immanent. Even in an age of science, it must partake of the religious, as we ourselves do, if it would understand us aright.

3

the creationist controversy

In January 1982, I had the honor of addressing the conference of the American Association for the Advancement of Science (AAAS) on the subject of creationism and biological science. I did not know, when I accepted this speaking engagement, that in December 1981 I would be a witness for the plaintiffs and the American Civil Liberties Union (ACLU) at the creationist trial in Little Rock, Arkansas. Participation in this trial enlightened me a good deal on the issues involved in this controversy, and a return to the creationist and the plaintiff cases, as one participant saw them, may provide the most clarifying entrance into the exceedingly complex interrelations of inquiry and belief in our present society.

Act 590, which was being challenged in federal court in Little Rock, called for "balanced treatment" in science classes (roughly "equal time") between what was called evolution science and creation science. The law specified that no references to "religious doctrines" or "religious materials" were to be made; it tried to define very broadly each of these "scientific models," as it called them; and it said that whenever either one was taught, then the other should also be taught. The law made no mention of either God or the book of Genesis. Nevertheless, in its definition of creation science, it listed as the elements of that model the sudden creation of all things out of nothing; the creation of separate and distinct "kinds" at the beginning; a catastrophic ("miraculous") interpretation of the earth's history; and the "recent" beginning of the universe, each of which elements requires for its intelligibility the notion of a supranatural creative act. The definition of creation science also asserted "the insufficiency of natural selection and mutations" to explain development, and "the naturalistic character" (read: "atheistic") of evolutionary science in the emergence of life and of the forms of life. The act declared its purpose to be that of ensuring "free debate" and "neutrality" in the teaching of origins by preventing the "dogmatic" teaching of *one* model (evolution) and so the establishment of theological liberalism or atheistic humanism. The subject of origins, the act said, is in fact taught, but only an evolutionary-naturalistic interpretation of origins is presented. Since this latter model is no self-evident "fact of science," an "alternative scientific model" should be presented if academic freedom for teachers and students alike is to be preserved. So much for the law.

On the face of it, this law seems innocent, even virtuous, enough. It pleads for objectivity and fairness, the rough justice of equal time. It promises to avoid religion; it seeks to break open a probably quite real liberal, humanistic establishment of ideas in the scientific and academic communities. Yet I am convinced that it is an exceedingly dangerous law, whose enactment to any wide extent would represent a disaster to our society. Why? Clearly the legal issue, as the ACLU lawyers saw, was that this law contravened the First Amendment. But there are also other, deeper issues involved. Although each of us would give a different emphasis to these elements, I suggest that the following represent the *main* reasons that defeat of this law is of such overriding importance.

1. The law endangers the free practice of religion in our society by the establishment in the public schools of one particular tradition (Christianity) and, further, one particular interpretation of the Christian religion. It does this by presenting as

"science" a particular, even sectarian, interpretation of the Christian symbol of creation and therefore of the book of Genesis, thus ruling out not only other religious and philosophical traditions than the Christian, but also other Christian views of creation, my own included. It tacitly equates religion and Christianity with a literalistic fundamentalism and this equation would be a disaster for the religious communities of America. This was the central reason most of the plaintiffs were church leaders and individual churchgoers, and why we witnesses from religious studies were present.

2. The law parades a model or theory as science that in fact is not science, and it inserts this theory into the scientific classroom. The result almost certainly will be either deep confusion about what science is and what theories most branches of contemporary science hold, or else the refusal to teach either model and so the disappearance of responsible science instruction in our secondary and high schools. This would in turn represent a disaster for American science as a whole, comparable to the fiasco of Soviet biology during the Lysenko era or of Chinese science during the Cultural Revolution. Our society is now technological to the core; such a society is certain to decline precipitously if the level of its scientific instruction is seriously damaged.

3. This law represents a dangerous challenge to academic freedom. Here not only is the State legislating on the subjects to be taught in a curriculum, it is going further and requiring a given profession—the science teachers—to teach certain definite theories or models. In doing this, the State replaces, or seeks to replace, the consensus of the community of working scientists as the authority capable of determining the methods and content of science: the scientifically legitimate "models" to be discussed and studied. No longer are the questions of what is science and what may be taught in its name to be answered by the community of scientists in the community's relation to the individual teacher of science (a relation that

can take a number of varied forms); instead it is answered au-
thoritatively by the State's insistence on these two theories and
no other. Expanded into other, even more sensitive areas such
as history, civics, political and economic theory, and philosophy, this precedent could well subvert the authority of each
professional community to determine its own criteria, canons,
or methods, and its subject matter, resulting in a disaster to
public education in our schools. According to our lawyers for
the creationist trial, this important, not to say crucial, element
of the case was too elusive legally or constitutionally to be made
central to our argument. As a result, it was more implied than
stressed in the presentation of our case.

Creationism

The basic error reflected in the law, and the cause of these three
potential disasters, was that these two models, one religious
(creationism) and the other scientific (evolution), were regarded
as equivalent, logically comparable, and thus mutually exclusive theories or interpretations. As the creationist documents
plainly show, both models are naively viewed as parallel explanations of "origins." Paradoxically, therefore, both were argued
to be on the one hand "scientific" or "equally scientific," and yet
on the other hand both are called equally "religious," the one in
this context representing a believing, Christian, and biblical religion and the other an "atheistic" or "humanistic" religion. If
one believed in evolution, one could not believe in God or the
Bible; correspondingly, if one believed in God and found some
sort of truth in Genesis, then in that case one must deny evolution. Only as equivalent hypotheses could both be regarded as
scientific explanations; only on this same ground could one be
regarded as the representative of valid religion (even if no religious words are mentioned); and only on this ground could the
State (in order to escape establishing "atheism") be viewed as
having a legitimate-seeming responsibility to make room for
both. This naive error of regarding evolution and Genesis as

comparable and therefore mutually exclusive "explanations" is not confined to the fundamentalist community, as we shall see in a moment. It represents, I suggest, *the* confusion out of which this controversy as a whole has arisen.

I was not able to be present when the State presented the case for the creationists and for this law. However, I have read extensively in the creation science literature and the briefs of the creationists' lawyers, and so I have a fairly good grasp of the implicit theological, philosophical, scientific, and legal logic of their case. The following two points, descriptive of the creationists' arguments, contain innumerable further confusions not only about religion but more especially about science, particularly about its formal structure, its methods, and its canons.

First, they claimed that creationism was not religion at all but science, a "scientific model," as they put it, based on "scientific evidence" or "scientific facts" and thus "at least as scientific as evolution." It was, they argued, not religion because it neither appealed to scriptural or doctrinal authority nor did it talk about God "religiously," that is, as personal, loving, a savior, and so on. Next their argument took a slightly different turn: neither creation nor evolution, they said, could be "scientifically proved," since origins, however interpreted, lie beyond direct observation and so beyond experimental testing. Thus the status of the two models is logically an equivalent one: the relative status of each depends on (1) the "scientific evidence" to which each can appeal, and (2) the capacity of each model to "explain intelligibly" these data. At this point, they expressed complete confidence in their own case as decently arguable on any platform, as presenting an authentically "scientific"—"rational"—explanation of origins based on empirical evidence.

Second, all of their writings, and the law itself, assumed that what they called a "naturalistic explanation," and thus any theory of science based on such an explanation, was inherently atheistic. If it leaves out God—as the scientific theory of evolution certainly does—then it is clearly false and so cannot be *really* science. (One can here see how in a scientific culture science is regarded not only as *true* but more as *defining truth.* As a consequence, to the religious people in such a culture, an atheistic science must ipso facto not be science but *false science;* they do *not* say—as in another age they might well have—that science is false but that this is false science.) Evolution, therefore, to them meant not merely a tentative theory full of empirical or scientific "holes"; it represented a deliberate and powerful expression of naturalism or atheism, an essentially antireligious viewpoint. And in some of their extracurricular (religious) writings, these same authors portrayed evolution as an instrument of aggression by cosmic forces of evil against the human race comparable to the horrors of the United Nations, the Equal Rights Amendment, international communism, and the Word Council of Churches! Again, a theoretical confusion about the nature of science and its relation to religion (which we shall take up below) was at the heart of, and made possible, their bizarre case. Seldom has a legal or constitutional error (and I assume it is that) so blatantly been dependent on a set of theoretical confusions, in the philosophy of science, the philosophy of religion, and in theology. It made Michael Ruse, the philosopher of science at the trial, and me, the philosopher of religion and theologian there, almost feel we each enjoyed a publicly useful, as well as an esoterically interesting, role!

What sorts of confusions are represented here? First, there is confusion about science, about what science is. They kept speaking of "scientific facts" and "scientific evidence," never of scientific theories. This is, I think, ignorance as well as guile, probably a bit of both. They—and recall, "they" are trained scientists—thought science was, so to speak, located in its facts. Michael and I agreed that, on the contrary, science was located in its theories, in its theoretical structure. Consequently (and conveniently for their argument), they had no conception of, or at least they never mentioned what are called, the "canons" of scientific method, its rules of the road, the logical conditions that make a theory a part of *science*. They seemed to think that if you marshaled empirical evidence for a theory, if it fitted and so explained "the facts," then it was scientific—even if it meanwhile appealed to a supranatural agent as cause, if it explained origins in terms of purposes, and if it culminated not in a statement of a universal law but in the appeal to a unique and unrepeatable event whose causal factors lay far beyond any possible observation or repeatable experimental testing. Their model, as a consequence, was in fact not an example of science at all: it involved a supranatural cause, transcendent to the system of finite causes; it explained in terms of purposes and intentions; and it cited a transcendent, unique, and unrepeatable (even in principle, uncontrollable) action. It represented, therefore, logically and linguistically a re-edition of a familiar form of thinking or explaining—one more theological or philosophical than scientific in procedure, one usually called "natural theology"—and an argument in which data of some sort are argued to point "rationally" to a philosophical-religious conclusion, namely, the agency of a divine being.

Second, the creationists failed to distinguish the question of *ultimate* origins: Where did it *all* come from? From the quite different question or questions of *proximate* origins: how did A arise out of B, if it did; or Q from P? Or, putting this point in the helpful categories of scholastic thought, they ignored the distinction (interestingly, ignoring this is a typical *modern* fallacy) between the *primary* causality of a First Cause, with which philosophy or theology might deal (Where did it *all* come from?), and *secondary* causality, causality confined to finite factors (for example, how did present forms of life arise out of *other* forms of life?). Again, assuming simply that it was the role of science to deal with the truth and therefore with *all* of the truth, they concluded that a scientific explanation of origins must be an *exhaustive* explanation and, so, inclusive of all possible factors or causes in any way involved. Thus, if evolutionary science deals with proximate origins, it must at the same time be dealing with the question of ultimate origins. If, therefore, in this process evolutionary theory has left out God, it must by that fact be asserting that there is no God, that the divine is in no way the creator of the process of secondary causes. To them, as a consequence, the demurral of the scientific witnesses that "science does not raise the question about God at all" meant in effect that science rules out the presence of God in any way and is therefore atheistic. (As we shall note, many scientists agree with them on this point!)

Obviously, here the creationists have ignored, or possibly been unaware of, the restrictive canons of the scientific method (for example, that no supernatural causes may be included in a theory) and the distinction of ultimate from proximate origins. As a consequence, they have failed, as do many, to understand the methodological *limits* of science, that while it provides testable and thus relatively certain conclusions, by the same token its conclusions or answers are limited and not exhaustive. Thus, as in the parallel cases of historical inquiry, of law, or of psychology, the so-called atheism of natural science is a priori and methodological. No acceptable historical or legal hypotheses can include the divine as a central cause of a historical event or a crime. If, as another example, objective psychological inquiry cannot locate experimentally (behavioristically) any sign of my inward freedom, this does not mean either that that freedom is not in fact there or that psychological inquiry denies human intentionality—unless, of course, one specifies in advance that *only* what is found by such inquiry is to be considered "real." In the same way, scientific explanations of proximate origins are confined to using *finite* causes as principles of explanation and thus leave quite open the question of God. As a consequence, the charge that evolution is "atheistic" is a simple tautology, an analytic judgment equivalent to the assertion "this is a scientific theory."

Note again how confusions about the nature and rules of the scientific method, about the distinction between scientific and other forms of knowing, and so about the limitations of scientific inquiry—and the subsequent distinction of ultimate from proximate questions of origins—have bred the theoretical confusions that have made this case possible. I repeat, these same confusions are not confined to fundamentalist groups. To a culture in which science represents the paradigmatic, if not the exclusive, mode of knowing, knowledge is apt to be regarded as all on one level. As a consequence, scientific explanations and religious explanations (so long as the latter are still taken seriously) are bound to conflict. And, as in this case, both will be regarded at one moment as "science" and at another as "religion." As much naturalistic humanism parades itself as "what we scientists now know," so in the same way its opposite number, fundamentalist creationism, challenges evolutionary science with the claim to represent an *alternative* "science." Which one is more confused about both science and religion is hard to say.

A "Scientific" Defense

The logic of the ACLU case was, of course, directed at these confusions embodied in the law itself and in this "scientific" defense of the law. It was an impressive case assembled by the lawyers for the ACLU in the name of the plaintiffs: the mainline churches, the National Association of Biology Teachers, three national Jewish groups, and interested individuals in Arkansas. There were four experts in the field of religion: a Catholic biblical scholar, a historian of fundamentalism, a sociologist of fundamentalism, and me, a theologian-philosopher. On the scientific side were a philosopher of science, a geneticist, a geologist, a microbiologist, and a paleontologist. Then came some very impressive teachers and administrators in the educational system of Arkansas, whose testimony I was not able to hear.

Because we saw the law as primarily contravening the First Amendment, we wished to establish first of all that creation science, the creationist model, represents "religion," and more, a particular form of religion, a form exclusive not only of all non-Christian religions but also of most recognized forms of Christian faith. Hence the presence at the start of our "religious" witnesses: a Methodist bishop, a Catholic biblical scholar who showed the sources of the creationist model in Genesis, a historian of fundamentalism who linked it up with the historic emphases of fundamentalism, and so on.

My own testimony dealt with the issue *theoretically*. In a monotheistic religion, I argued, and so in a monotheistic culture, all that is religious has to do with God (thou shalt worship no other gods but me!), and conversely, all that has to do with God is religious. For monotheistic religions, God is the principle of ultimate reality, and so the source of all other reality; the principle of authority in revelation; the source of every religious way of life; and the founding agent of the religious community. Religion here is referent essentially and exclusively to God. This religious reference includes *all* of God's actions, his or her creative activity in establishing the world as well as the divine redeeming action in reuniting with us. For this reason, all supranatural beings who create are "gods" as much as all such beings who save. To speak of a creator of all things, therefore, is to speak religiously, even if a philosophical argument may also be produced to give secular warrants for this notion. Not all religions have gods and surely not all worship God, but all that has to do with God is certainly religious. When, in order to circumvent this argument, the State sought to separate the Creator implied by creation science from "religion," and so from the God who saves, they were, I pointed out, coming close thereby to the first and worst Christian heresy, namely, the denial of monotheism—the belief in two gods, one of them the morally dubious creator and the other the good, loving Savior God. It was, I argued, no accident at all that the first article of the earliest Christian creed was also the first book of the Scriptures, witnessed to one God, the Father Almighty, the Maker of heaven and earth.

Further, if religious statements are referent to God and not to finite causes—and this defines religious assertions in the West—then of all the statements about God that could be made, the proposition that God creates "out of nothing" is the *most* religious. By definition, no other agent was present since this act established all other agents; only God acts and so God is the *only* possible subject of the proposition—whereas in even the incarnation, as orthodoxy understood it, Mary was also present and in some measure active. The law, therefore, is religious not because it refers explicitly to a doctrine or appeals to Scripture; it is religious because essential to each of the constitutive elements of the creationist model is the notion of the agency of a supranatural being, of God—and that is ipso facto religious speech. Finally, this is a *particular* religious view of creation, different from that of other religious traditions and different from other Christian interpretations. Essentially, it is not a scientific model at all but a theological one, and thus it contravenes the First Amendment.

Subsequent testimony by the distinguished panel of scientists continued this line of argument. This is not, said they, science at all, and they sought to show why. Moreover, so they argued, in making its own case as legitimate science, creationism has misunderstood—if it did not deliberately misrepresent (and the evidence for that latter was stacked very high in the courtroom!)—the methods of science, many of its fundamental laws (for example, the second law of thermodynamics), and many of its present theoretical conclusions. In denying that evolution is valid science, in asserting that it is, in fact, disguised religion, and in rejecting the testability of its major conclusions, the creation scientists reveal that they do not in fact understand how the relevant sciences proceed, how their theories are composed and tested, and what a firm status in the whole of science these hypotheses can rightly claim. To make these arguments, an awesome lineup of scientists appeared: Ayala the geneticist, Dalrymple the geologist, Murowitz the microbiologist, and Gould the paleontologist. They proffered devastating testimony, in effect four lectures covering a wide swath of contemporary science, its procedures and its relatively reliable conclusions concerning the age of the earth and its system, the origins of life, genetic mutation and development, and the paleontological record. Cross-examination of these imposing experts was by no means easy, even for the cleverest of lawyers. Mostly they were asked about rival theories (for example, the weird conjectures of Messrs. Hoyle and Crick concerning the origin of life); about gaps, fissures, and controversies in evolutionary theory; and whether our witnesses as representatives of "the scientific establishment" felt teachers should be free to teach deviant or heterodox theories—and if so, why not creation science? There is, of course, precious little consensus on the issue of origins; consequently, this area represented a fertile field for sharp cross-examination. It is interesting to note that the distinction between alternative *scientific* accounts and a *religious* account of origins was fundamental to the defense of each of our scientific witnesses against this line of questioning. Time and again the answer was "but *that* is not science"—an answer dependent for its force on the mostly unexplicated distinction between scientific and religious speech and understanding, a distinction operative in types of questions asked, in procedures and authorities invoked, and in the forms of speech used and the shape of the resulting systems of symbols.

The Deeper Issues

It is now time to scan briefly the deeper issues at the interface of inquiry and belief embodied in this case. First, it is clear that this case does not represent a simple warfare between the enlightened forces of science on the one hand and the darkening forces of religion on the other, as is frequently implied by fundamentalists, by the secular intelligentsia, and by the media. The makeup of the list of plaintiffs and their witnesses shows this. Almost all the mainline churches were represented on the "science" side and only *one* scientific organization, and on our own team half the witnesses represented religion. On the other hand, for the defense of creatiohism, a whole battery of "scientists" provided the theoretical backing and gave the central testimony. The opposition boasted several score of scientists with advanced degrees in science from major universities. They could not, I warrant, have found a single biblical scholar or theologian with the same level of professional degree to support them. If one then says, "But these are not recognized, established scientists, working members of the scientific community," one can answer, neither were the spokesmen for the type of religion represented by the creationists "recognized, established" religious leaders. None of *them* could or would conceivably ever be found in the membership of the American Theological Society, the American Academy of Religion, or the National Council of Churches! The image of a warfare of science versus religion was, as historians of science now recognize, even untrue to the real situation of the nineteenth century.

Now this picture of a conflict between two separate forces: old-time religion and new-world science, is, in our advanced technological culture, sheer mythology. Technology and science in some form or other now characterize *all* levels of society, and correspondingly, so do "faith" and the religious in some sense or other. Moreover, the religion represented here is itself a function, a product, or an aspect of that technological and scientific society, not a carryover from the old. Fundamentalist and cultic forms of religion have grown in our lifetime *because of* the dilemmas of a technological society, not *despite* the character of that society. Both technology and religion are permanent and essential aspects of the culture as a whole; both are potentially very creative as well as potentially infinitely destructive. The comprehension of *science* among the general population and the population's evaluation of the uses of *technology* are hardly profound, nor are they acceptable to members of the AAAS. Correspondingly, the interpretation and use of *religion* by much of the population at large leave in the eyes of the established and professional religious and theological communities much to be desired, though, let us remember, the elite in either realm are by no means the exclusive bearers either of intelligence and skill or of persevering faith, compassion, and courage.

As an addendum, let me say that I was deeply surprised to find that only the National Association of Biology Teachers— not geologists, the astrophysicists, and the AAAS itself—were represented among the plaintiffs. Just as this case is important for the defense of religious pluralism and of creative religion in the modern setting, so it is also vital to the defense of scientific excellence in our cultural life. It is surely time that the powerful forces of science officially share the burden of this matter with the churches and the ACLU.

If this is not, then, merely the last episode in a continuing warfare between two distinguishable groups—religion and science—but, in fact, the much more complex problem of the misinterpretation on many levels of two essential and pervasive aspects of our cultural life, where and how does the problem arise? How are we to understand this problem and this case? First, it is surely clear that a vast amount of blame rests with the churches and the schools of theology. One of the major tasks of theology in the modern period has been to understand reflectively how religious faith, and therefore how Christian religious faith, even faith in Genesis, can be reinterpreted and represented in the light of modern science within the framework of the theoretical *Weltanschauung* in which, in a scientific age, we actually live our lives. This has been variously done with modest success for nearly two hundred years. Yet clearly this has not been taught or communicated forcefully or persistently enough either in theological schools or in the churches. A satisfactory, intelligible understanding of the relation of religion and science has not permeated even into church life, much less into American society as a whole. Many, if not most, people still assume—and these people are not only the fundamentalists—that to believe in God or the Bible one must reject evolution. For example, when I had just stepped out of the witness box in Little Rock, a *Time* reporter asked me in bafflement, "If you are a Christian theologian and believe in revelation, how can you accept Darwin?" I replied, "On many counts I don't. I understand there are today a number of scientific reasons for questioning elements of Darwin's theory." The reporter was still baffled.

The responsibility of the religious community is clear enough, and I would like to stress that point. What is not so obvious to all is the responsibility, as well, as of the scientific community for this same problem. In the first place, a goodly number of scientists, some exceedingly prominent, share with the fundamentalists the confusion noted earlier, namely, that scientific knowledge simply replaces and dissolves religious myth. Religion here is viewed—as is quite natural by a scientific culture and especially by academics—as primarily "belief," an early and very shaky stage of the human enterprise of *cognition*, of understanding the world around us: an enterprise that (flatteringly enough) reaches its culmination with us, specifically in modern science. Religion, therefore, is understood as "pre-science," "early science," "primitive science"; it can, therefore, be expected to vanish, as do all denizens of the night, when the daylight of science appears and spreads—a view often called the "Walt Disney theory" of cultural history. If, then, secularists as well as fundamentalists see science as *replacing* religious views, the significant difference is that while the sophisticated scientists reject *all* of religion as pre-science, the creationists at some point dig in their heels and hang onto certain doctrines associated with their religious faith, thus rejecting those particular individual scientific hypotheses that to them compete with the doctrines of that faith. One encounters this understanding of science as dissolving religious truth on the scientific side in Julian Huxley and Gaylord Simpson. One heard it repeatedly from Jacob Bronowski, and one sees it on TV from our most distinguished scientific popularizers. A recent volume of readings in evolutionary theory edited by C. Leon Harris classifies Genesis under the heading of "pre-scientific myth" and cites the great Augustine under the bizarre title "The Infanticide of Science: Augustine and the Dark Ages." This is about as informed and sensitive as to what Genesis and Augustine were about as listing Einstein and Fermi under the heading "The development of destructive weaponry."

One could go on and on with examples of this basic agreement of many within the scientific community with the creationists: truth, if there be truth, is all on one level, and as a consequence, Genesis and modern science directly compete and so replace each other. Thus for the creationists, Genesis can be the source for an "alternative science"; thus also are scientific hypotheses conceived by many scientists and their followers as replacing and dissolving what used to be called religious truth or a "mythical understanding of reality." The great Harlow Shapley, toward the end of his life, lectured repeatedly on the theme: "As a scientist I now know there is no God; there is only the blind universe—but what a universe!" It was impressive cosmic mysticism that he here so forcefully preached, but it was *not* science. And he was quite as naively unaware of this as is Dr. Duane Gish when he claims "as a scientist" to have established what is in fact the Genesis account of origins.

Not only is there the theoretical agreement here between the scientific naturalists and the fundamentalists that religious truth and scientific theory are direct competitors and therefore mutually exclusive. On the practical level, one tends to breed and encourage the other in a strange and unfortunate evolutionary development. As the biographies of many modern disdainers of religions show, much of scientific naturalism has gestated out of parental fundamentalism or orthodoxy. Correspondingly, this new fundamentalist reaction against evolution arises in significant part because of the frequently careless and uninformed way evolutionary science has been taught. Each time a child comes home and reports, "I learned in science class today that Genesis is wrong," the seed is planted for the creationist reaction. As fundamentalism originally arose in the late nineteenth and early twentieth centuries as a reaction against liberal and modernist Protestantism, so creation science has arisen in our day in reaction to scientific naturalism, a global and "religious" worldview based on science but going far beyond science itself to encompass all of experience and to give that total experience a framework of intelligible meaning.

As in the earlier case of theology, there is here, as perhaps the one correctable element, a failure in education—in this instance, a failure in education of scientists. As the scores of scientists supporting the creationist movement indicate, many trained scientists have little understanding even of *science*. As we noted, they locate science in its facts and evidences but are unaware of the meaning of scientific observation and falsification. They have no notion of the requirements or canons of the necessary theoretical structure if a hypothesis is to be called "scientific." Apparently the philosophy of science—reflective concentration on the method, the logical structure, the extent, and the limits of science—has only rarely been a part of the education of scientists. For that lack, the community of science is clearly now paying dearly.

It is rightly taken for granted in a scientific culture that the modern educated person—be he or she academic humanist, theologian, lawyer, legislator, minister, doctor, or what-have-you—should in some measure understand science, at least enough to be cognizant of its methods (and its limits!), of its most general conclusions, and above all of the "world" of reality, truth, and value that it has implied and continues to imply. On the other hand, because, I suspect, of the myth of

the absoluteness and self-sufficiency of scientific knowing and
a confidence in the imminent disappearance of religion, the reverse has not been the case. Scientists all too often have not
been expected, nor expected it from themselves, to be *fully*
aware of the wider implications of their own methods for the
rest of life. Especially they have not been encouraged to reflect
on the relations of *their* truth to *other* ways of knowing, to the
"truth" embodied in historical inquiry, in art, in morals, in
philosophy, and in religion. Other disciplines surely should be
aware of the science at the heart of our culture, but it is
equally fatal if those at that center are unable to reflect creatively on the relation of that scientific center to the rest of our
cultural life.

As a consequence, the lack of understanding, even in some
cases of knowledge, of other important aspects of our cultural
life, is often surprising. Two very intelligent and well-informed
teachers of general science at the University of Chicago Labora-
tory School, who worried that the father of one of their pupils
was a "theologian," wrote me a note saying that evolution and
primitive anthropology were about to be taught in my son's class
and, wanting to be fair to all, they cordially invited me to visit
the class to explain how we (meaning the University of Chicago
Divinity School, the recognized mother of modernist theology!)
practice "biblical dating"! When I replied giving a short history
of two hundred years of biblical criticism, of liberal religion, and
of the University of Chicago Divinity School, and offering some
relevant theological reinterpretations thereof, they replied, "This
is marvelous, courageous, and far-out stuff—why don't you put
it into an article for publication?"—not in the slightest aware of
the literally tons of scholarly literature on these themes. Both of
them were delighted, though still somewhat puzzled, that I went
to Little Rock, as they said, on the "right side."

The myth that religion will vanish in a secular and scientific culture—and so any study of religion is on a par with careful reflection on the implications of astrology or magic—is itself

vanishing under the pressure of repeated historical falsification. Part of the counterfactual data to this myth about the
demise of religion is the reappearance in new power of fundamentalism. Part of that data is represented by the appearance
in unexpected variety and strength of non-Western religious
cults. Part of it is the appearance at the center of politics and
economics of ideologies or myths about history that unify, em-
power, and direct modern technological societies much as
traditional religions unified and directed archaic societies—for
example, the myth of democratic, liberal, and scientific
progress on the one hand and the myth of Marxist communism
on the other. None of these new emergents, appearing suddenly
and unexpectedly in our lifetime, represent traditional religion,
carryovers from the past, as certainly do the Christian and Jewish congregations in the West. These new forms of the religious
have appeared and reappeared *out of* and *because of* a scientific, technological culture. First, all of this is there (as it always
is) in response to the ever-present and essential demand for a
credible system of symbols giving structure, meaning, and direction to all of experience: to nature, history, society, and the
self. Second, it has surfaced in response to the particular and
very sharp anxieties, not to say terrors, of a technological age,
especially one in marked, though probably not yet admitted,
decline.

One of the lessons our age has taught us is that scientific
knowledge and the technology it makes possible are not, as were
once believed, purely benevolent. Rather they can both be terri-
bly ambiguous, creative of evil as well as of good, instruments of
self-destruction as well as of survival. Thus are they and their
use *dependent* on other aspects of culture: on its political and
legal structures and processes, its moral integrity and courage,
and the forms of its religious faith. Correspondingly, as I have
here argued and as this case shows, our era has also shown the
persistence, the permanence, and the ever-renewed power, as
well as the deep ambiguity, of religion. Modern secular culture

had been thoroughly aware of that ambiguity; it has long looked at religion with suspicion and looked forward to its demise. What, therefore, it had not accepted, and probably still does not accept, is that persistence. But religion in one form or another—and its forms are almost infinitely various—is and will be there, like science, and it will be there in demonic or in creative form. Thus the relations between these two essential and permanent elements of culture represent a recurrent and foundational problem. It is, therefore, an issue on which each of our communities—the religious and the scientific—should be informed, about which each should reflect, and to which the training of each should in part be directed. Critical and reflective interpretation of *both* science and profound religion should be as much a part of the self-understanding of the scientist as of the religionist. If such self-reflective and critical interrelation is not the case, if significant religious groups fail to understand science, and if large segments of the scientific community ignore or misinterpret religion—as illustrated in this trial—then religion will not thereby wither and die. We can only expect that, in that case, a scientific and technological culture whose intellectual leaders refuse to reflect on the religious will find itself in the end ruled and directed by an irrational, not to say demonic, *form* of the religious—as in the case of Nazi Germany or Stalinist Russia.

In a time of troubles such as we are entering, the religious dimension tends to expand and, unfortunately, to grow in fanaticism, intolerance, and violence; science and technology tend accordingly to concentrate more and more on developing greater and greater means to destructive and repressive power. This combination represents a most dependable recipe for self-destruction. Let each of our communities, the scientific and the religious—and quite possibly, the academic as well—rethink its own role in this light and especially its relations to the other community in our total social life. Only then can we prevent the proliferation of laws such as this one that unite science and religion in ways destructive of the genius of each. Science and religion *will* unite in some form or another in any case: in theocratic or fundamentalist form, in political, ideological form—or in the more desirable form of a relation respectful of the autonomy and yet the creative power of each. Such a desideratum, however, requires critical reflection *both* ways, dialogue between us *both*, joint deliberation and, above all, mutual respect, interest, and forbearance. It is not too late for these two important communities to embark on such mutually vital communication. Let us begin.

4

the religious right

Our subject is the Religious Right, a large, amorphous, and growing group of American Christians that represents theologically a fundamentalist interpretation of Christianity—I prefer the word *fundamentalist* to *evangelical*, since the latter is a much wider term—and is active politically largely through the Christian Coalition. I need not remind you how important they are in present American political life. They are a prime example of an explicit union of religious faith and loyalty with political policy and action. We shall reflect on them largely as a religious rather than a sociological phenomenon, that is, as a religious group deliberately and successfully seeking political authority and power. It is, however, well to remember that such unions of religion and politics also have important secular results—consequences for the shape of ordinary secular life—regarding the terms of debate in ordinary, secular affairs, and so regarding the character of wider American culture.

Two examples among many will show the importance of these secular effects: (1) The denial of the authority of science on scientific subjects (or of history or social science) in the name of religious truth—for example, creation science. Here revelation replaces scientific inquiry within the domain of science, reshapes scientific conclusions, and overrules scientific education. In effect, this is the elimination of science. (2) The

43

denial of open and rational reflection in other social matters—
in the areas of law, economics, politics, morals, and, of course,
religion. The essence of fundamentalism is its claim to absolute
truth; in turn, a politically aggressive fundamentalism expands
this claim outward from the areas of personal religion and
morals (as in historic fundamentalism) to all matters in society
generally. If the use of reason in wider cultural life means and
requires open criticism, debate, and reflection, reason here has
effectively vanished. At best, reason can now serve only a particular creed, moral code, and style of life; as a questioning,
constructive, and thus creative factor in culture, reason has
succumbed.

   This interweaving of religion and politics is not new. Nor
can the two ever be completely sundered. A close union of the
two has persisted during most of human history, a union de-
nounced, ironically, by the Baptist tradition—perhaps the
major supporters of the present Religious Right. Although such
an interweaving of religious doctrine and morals with political
power, political policies, and public law seems strange, even
abnormal, to us, we should recognize that in history this sort
of union has been almost universal, more a normal character
of historic societies than not. This is true whether we look at
primordial tribal groups, at ancient societies, at the medieval
Catholic world, or at most early Protestant nations. The so-
called "separation" in the eighteenth century of these two
factors present in all social life was a radically new departure,
scandalizing many amazed onlookers at the time.

   However we may now feel about such unions, moreover,
there are important social and religious factors that press toward such interweaving—and thus that must continually be
restrained. Each community has significant presuppositions
about the world as a whole and human life within it that make
its common social and cultural life possible. These border on
the religious. They are expressed in symbols, and they are
communally held by inner assent or participation—as one

participates in the "spirit" of one's nation, its values, goals, and ideals. These commonly held presuppositions represent for that community the source for its understanding of itself, of its world, of ideal human being and human society, and so they provide the bases for its most important political and social goals and policies, and for its common roles and tasks, its vocations, its norms and ideals for life; and finally they provide meaning, grounds for courage, confidence, and hope for the common future. These are, as we said, "religious" in the broadest sense, and they are fundamental for all serious politics. Most important political speech is about those presuppositions, a renewed expression of them. When they seem to dissolve away, it is at once a religious and a political crisis, and that void must be rectified by some renewal of the common faith and common standards. We are at present experiencing such a sense of deep loss. Hence just as the religious tends toward public, social as well as private, individual enactment, so inevitably the political tends toward the religious.

The Claim to Absolute Religious Truth

Most important in the union of fundamentalist Christianity and politics is the claim of fundamentalism to *absolute* religious truth, to possessing *the* gospel, the only true Christianity, or, as one fundamentalist Christian put it, "God's religion." This means that to them, their religious and moral agenda represents an absolute moral obligation for everyone, a universal requirement. It also means that all else united in their minds with this understanding of religion shares in this absoluteness. Hence arises the identification of their own particular political, social, economic, and moral stance with authentic Christianity and so with the same absoluteness. Their views of social matters become "Christian" views of such issues, and no alternative views are tolerated: "dissenters cannot really be Christian." As a consequence, there follows the point we made earlier, namely, the denial of the openness of public debate and of culture, concerning art, literature, law, science—in the end, this is the denial of thought itself.

There is here a striking difference with nonfundamentalist forms of Christianity and Judaism, which, while affirming the validity and importance of their own positions, nonetheless recognize their own as one perspective among others. In their case, their particular political, economic, and social stance does not receive absolute authentication; political, moral, and religious diversity, if not applauded, is recognized and accepted. When, however, American religious fundamentalism unites with the political, then inevitably certain aspects of present American culture, which they regard as "true American" and "true Christianity," are also made absolute. What is error to them begins to have no right.

Religion concerns the absolute; it represents a relation to something transcendent and ultimate. Inwardly, therefore, it expresses itself, as Paul Tillich said, as ultimate concern. This relation to transcendence can in human social life be very creative, giving ultimate goals and standards to life and yet providing the grounds for the criticism, the judgment, and so the self-criticism necessary for us all (what has been called the "prophetic principle"). As history shows, however, religion is also risky. Our own interpretation of faith, of God's will for ourselves and others, can be identified with the divine object of faith, our own religion and moral canons with God and God's will. Religiously this identification of ourselves and our views with God is *idolatry;* when the same thing happens in secular political guise, it is *ideology.* Socially, both in effect mean *theocracy.* Hence the theocratic union of the religious and the political can be either secular-political or religious-political: a secular ideology claiming absolute authority, or a religious fundamentalism seeking political and social rule. Both were common in the twentieth century: in Japan, in Germany, in Communist Russia, in Shiite Iran.

As all this indicates, the ultimate aim of such a union is *theocracy:* the rule over civil society by one religious (or ideological) creed, by one religious moral law, and by one religious ruling class: "It is Christians who should rule the state (and the world)," or "Our aim is to make this Christian America."

This theocratic expansion of religion outward into control of civil society characterizes every present form of fundamentalism in the last decades, as it has most modern political ideologies. Formerly in our century, fundamentalism had been *apolitical;* it claimed absolute authority in religious and moral matters but only for its own. In the American context and because of the First Amendment, fundamentalism thus has seemed to be nice or tame (if a bit out of date). Now, however, it has moved out; it sees itself as representing Middle America, "normal America." And, as it admits, it has its eye on reinterpreting the First Amendment. As it now says, fundamentalism intends to make this a Christian nation: in creation science, in its social agenda, in its identification of its own political and economic views with real Christianity, and in its as yet implicit racism and sexism, as well as in its nostalgic yearning for an older America where diversity of religion (without the limitation of race) and lifestyle were not yet present, and where gender roles and responsibilities were crystal clear. Without the limitation of the First Amendment, if it marshals, for whatever cause, enough popular support, fundamentalism naturally drives toward theocracy. This is illustrated now among us but also elsewhere in our contemporary world, in Islam, in radically orthodox groups in Israel, in Buddhist Sri Lanka, in Hindu India, and most recently in Japanese sects. When politics becomes absolute, then there appears its implicit religious dimension; when religion claims absolute validity and seeks control over all of life, there is political theocracy.

The Establishment of Religion

We must remember that the establishment of religion is always the establishment of *somebody's* religion. Hence it is also the establishment of some particular religious ruling group. There can be no establishment of a "neutral, nonsectarian religion," as these groups claim. Even if all religious groups were theistic, which certainly they are not, a "neutral theism," when established politically and socially, would represent *somebody's* theism and not that of other citizens, certainly not that of nonbelievers as well as believers. As the prophetic tradition in the Bible recognized—and the Founding Fathers agreed—religion is risky unless certain definite limits are set: (1) it must be *self-limiting* by self-criticism, by the recognition of the partiality and even the fault of even its own embodiment of the truth by which it lives, and (2) it must be limited in civil society, as for example by the First Amendment or by the general "democratic" social practice of the tolerance of diversity, such as in Britain, Holland, and Canada.

This absolutist mind-set—whether in religious form or secular ideological form—to our surprise has in the last century taken into itself (and without much resistance!) science-based technology, theoretical science, medicine, and law. This marriage of science with religious or political fanaticism would have been considered quite impossible, even incredible, at the end of the nineteenth century. But in the Japan of the 1930s, in Nazi Germany, in Soviet Russia, and potentially at least in modern Iran and China, a union of fundamentalist ideology and science has repeatedly appeared. Our homegrown form of this unexpected union of fundamentalist religion and science is creation science, which claims to represent authentic science based on a literal reading of the book of Genesis. This is by no means a dead issue; a different Supreme Court could well open the door to this new mode of science. "Harmless and eccentric," say many conservative intellectuals, (I'm thinking of William Buckley and Robert Novak.) happy to have unexpected political allies. In fact, such a union is neither harmless nor eccentric; examples of ideology and science have frequently enough established themselves in power. If the Religious Right has its way, creation science will be the science taught in our schools, and the narratives of Adam and Eve, Cain and Abel and their progeny will constitute the history of humankind taught there! As Duane Gish, a prominent creationist, said to me after our debate in 1985: "You have academia, Gilkey; but I have the White House. In a decade we will have the Republican Party. When we move on further than these first few steps, creation science will be the science and biblical history the history and social studies taught in America." In other places and times—the Germany of the early 1930s, for example—political conservatives labeled as "merely eccentric" their new political allies against the liberalism both feared. But when those eccentrics came to power in Germany and Japan, their conservative allies were gobbled up as quickly as were the liberals.

I said a moment ago that the ultimate aim of this movement, sometimes explicitly stated but mostly implicit, is the establishment of theocracy, the rule over all of civil society according to one set of religious beliefs, to one code of religious morals, and in the end by one ruling caste. This attempt to reestablish theocracy after a century dominated by modern industry, technology, and science is one of history's great surprises. Yet it is that precise aim that is expressed by the phrase "Christian America" and defended as legitimate by their absurd myth of the "Bible faith" of the Founding Fathers. Although, as Robertson admits, their entire agenda may not now be politically feasible, that agenda represents their long-term goal, to be achieved, as Gish said, by the eventual capture of the Republican Party.

Needless to say, if civil society is directed according to one religious and moral code, those persons who do not share those beliefs become second-class citizens. Of course, in every historical theocracy there remained dissenting members who rejected, mostly silently, the faith of the ruling majority, but in all such societies "nonbelievers" were denied equal social, economic, and political status. As we noted, the establishment of religion is the establishment in power, in prestige, and in opportunity of only *one* community in the wider society, namely, those who share that particular faith. This the Founders knew well; the establishment of religion represented to them the corruption of religion (William Penn and Roger Williams) and the corruption of the state (James Madison and Thomas Jefferson)—it also would represent, as New Jersey argued, the rule over New Jersey either by Anglican Virginia or Puritan Massachusetts! This is why the Founders took special care in the First Amendment to protect the religious minority against domination by precisely the religious majority.

Elements of Truth in Other Traditions

Every view of Christianity (or of Judaism, Islam, or Buddhism) grasps some important elements of that tradition's truth and tends to omit or downplay some elements. While all forms of Christianity, for example, hold themselves to be related to the absoluteness of God, none of these interpretations is itself absolute, and arguably each can learn much from the other perspectives: Orthodox, Roman, Anglican, Protestant, Evangelical, Pentecostal, liberal. Most of mainline Christianity, for example, has ignored creative elements of the Christian tradition that conservative Christianity has preserved: an emphasis on personal morality, a recognition of the danger of "vices," an appreciation of the saving power of repentance and of grace, and a sober consciousness of the reality of judgment and of death. On the other hand, liberals did center their concerns on other matters that were genuine and vital elements of the biblical tradition, elements that had been in their time ignored: the priority of *justice* as constitutive of any healthy, and certainly any Christian, community (love for neighbor in community means justice for all); the common *care* for those who suffer, who are underprivileged or oppressed ("And oppress not the widow, nor the fatherless, the stranger, nor the poor," Zech. 7:10); and a sharp, self-critical ("prophetic") *judgment* on their own religious community as well as on the injustices of the wider society.

These elements of so-called liberal Christianity represent New Testament values and are unquestionably authentically Christian. Further, they are basic for any so-called "family values"; there can be few viable families in a society characterized by great injustice. And the prominence of these "humanitarian" values in our democratic social tradition stems from their centrality in the common Judaic and Christian heritage of our social tradition. Thus these self-critical judgments on our society's economic and social injustices, as well as on its monetary greed, represent an authentic tradition of *religious* criticism of American culture. That critique began with the judgment on slavery and continued with critiques on unbridled predatory capitalism, on racial segregation, and on militant nationalism. Such criticism is surely "prophetic"; it is central to Old and New Testaments alike.

Little of this sort of critical stance vis-à-vis American modernity is, however, visible in fundamentalist Christianity; nor is much about justice heard from the Religious Right. Modern American fundamentalism does not stand apart from American culture, as it is so apt to claim. On the contrary, it has absorbed and united to itself important elements of contemporary culture. The Religious Right thus regards its emphasis on dogmatic fidelity, personal vices, sexual deviance, abortion, and what it holds to be the moral relativism and permissiveness of our society as constituting a full denunciation of "modernity." This is an illusion. The Religious Right's unconditioned championing of the rights of managers and property owners, its uncritical support of radical individual liberties, including the right to own all manner of weapons, its support of the nation's military and economic dominance, and its overt impatience with any attempts, however precarious, to establish a more equal society, a more peaceful world, or a more habitable planet represent an undeniable capitulation to some of present-day America's most dubious values. And it is precisely these very relative and debatable values that are called "authentically Christian" and so are absolutized.

Quite un-self-consciously, furthermore, the Religious Right uses the most modern technology based on the science it repudiates, and quite without reflection it supports the unlimited expansion of modern commercial dominance over the environment. In sum, it has uncritically incorporated into its own heart far more of the dubious aims and values of modern American life than has even mainline Christianity. Both represent modern, "relevant," and, by the same token, relative and partial interpretations of their common gospel. When, however, one of these identifies its version as absolute, as one with the truth of God, it thereby impoverishes itself, perverts the gospel, and will in the end lay waste the commonwealth. By pretending to be above culture, as it is not, it will destroy culture.

Finally, the teaching of this pseudoscience, creation science, either alongside legitimate sciences or in place of it, would seriously weaken the science—as well as the religion—on which technological society, including its military excellence, so clearly depends. Let us not forget that no missile or Air Force jet flies (not to mention a missile defense system!) without the most advanced sciences of physics and astronomy, nor is there any oil found without the science of geology. Thus the serious weakening or cessation of scientific education would in the end threaten our national security far more than any conceivable thefts of atomic secrets. If we wish to weaken ourselves militarily or industrially and hence endanger our national welfare and security, then the surest way to accomplish that is to replace the teaching of legitimate science with that of pseudoscientific theories. Granted this evident danger from pseudoscience, one can only wonder whether the slightest concern for their country's security, or general welfare, motivates those who press for creation science in our science class rooms. This is no mere conflict between varying religious beliefs and doctrines; on the contrary, it is my view that teaching creation science translates into a tremendously wounded industrial and military America.

Responses to Modern Culture

Modern culture, to its own surprise, apparently generates deep personal and communal anxieties. These arise from innumerable sources: developments in technology with their more obvious dangers; the spread of impersonal urbanization; the loss of the certainty of progress both for individuals and families and for America generally; the challenge of diverse, relativistic, and secular culture to treasured (and heretofore dominant) moral absolutes and religious convictions—and on and on. As any commentator knows, all of this has resulted in a widespread sense of lostness, of loneliness, of alienation, of a lack of self-direction and meaning, of not knowing either where we are going or whether we will get there. In short, it results in the loss of an overarching scheme of meaning that tells us who we are in the nature of things and that gives purpose and hope to our lives, whether that scheme be religious or progressivist—and it was usually both, *and both* are threatened. Because of this onset of anxiety in (or because of) a modern, industrial age, religion has not at all dwindled (as was earlier expected) but has continued and prospered, especially conservative religion.

Further, a scientific culture tends to snuff out as meaningless and futile serious discourse that is not "scientific," and hence to question the authenticity of rational, moral, and religious reflection. For much of our business, political, and academic leadership, all we need is science, engineering, industrial, and commercial know-how and some modest humanist ideals. The wider presuppositions of any creative culture, and especially of a modern scheme of norms and of meaning, simply do not exist. Hence responsible debate about them, about the character of reality and the grounding of meaning, debate that would

reground and reshape these presuppositions, is not possible.
Thus deep anxieties about our world and ourselves, anxieties
that must be answered, are not answered reflectively. On the
contrary, they are dealt with by irrational, illiberal, absolutist
forms of politics, morals, and religion. As Tillich said, the dissolution of a confident "scientific" autonomy leads to the appearance of a religious heteronomy or authoritarianism. Ironically,
a modern rational, scientific, technological culture, by its enthu-
siasm for its own "foundationless" status, seems to be in the
process of breeding its own opposite. It seems to be breeding a
"patricide"—a form of religion that would eliminate the essential
structures that have given birth to and supported all that is creative in that very culture.

An aggressive, modern form of fundamentalism is,
therefore, probably part of our immediate future, and so, as a
consequence, is the threat of its lurking companion, theocracy.
Republicans who are politically astute had best be careful lest
in co-opting the Religious Right for the sake of their own party,
they may in the end be used for a theocratic agenda that they
may now view as merely a bizarre irritation. The European
Left had to admit in the 1950s that there could be "enemies on
the left"—this seems obvious to us now. Still, conservative
forces in this country seem to recognize no possibility of "an
enemy on the right." Even more, religious leaders, at present
standing silently by in horrified disapproval (silent because
afraid to alienate people from their own religious communities), must pluck up their courage, dust off their own deepest
convictions, and declare their minds—theologically, religiously,
morally, and politically. Religion and politics, while distinct,
can probably never be separated—nor should they. Almost
certainly, some mode of the religious will always unite with the
political, sometimes in creative and sometimes in vastly destructive ways. Thus the point is *how* in each epoch they are brought
into union, whether in dogmatic, absolutist form or whether with
conviction tempered by humility and self-criticism.

5

the meaning and relevance of creation

The meaning and relevance of creation has a great deal to do with the relation of our common religious faith to contemporary science, and I will try to spell out the interesting complexity of that relation. The first place to look is the Book of Genesis, and my special topic is the present relevance of this opening book of the Hebrew and Christian Scriptures. I shall, moreover, limit my remarks even further and concentrate our thoughts on the first two chapters: the magnificent hymn to origins, or as we like to call it, the creation. Of course, the third chapter on the temptation and fall of Adam and Eve, and the fourth on the "wages of sin," as the King James has it, are also, or even more, of contemporary relevance, as each day's newspaper vividly illustrates. There is, however, far too much of sin and its consequences, both in our recent past and in our present, to be described today. In any case, Genesis is a text the history of whose meaning has formed the entire tradition of our cultural life—and these meanings continue to shape our own reactions to each new event.

I wish, however, to focus only on creation, or origins, the substance of the first two chapters. For though these chapters of Genesis represent a fairly obscure and enigmatic text from the ancient world of the so-called Near East in the eighth to the fifth centuries B.C.E., these chapters are in a number of ways

very relevant to us: to our religion, our personal piety, and our
theology; even more, they are significant for the deepest assumptions or presuppositions of our wider, secular cultural
life in the West; and not least, they have provided important
bases for the enterprise of modern science. Most surprisingly,
in the last decades they have become central also to our present legal and political existence. It is with this latter political
and legal relevance that I wish to begin.

The Creationists

When Genesis appears in our present consciousness, or in the
news, it probably connotes issues inspired by the creationists,
arguments in which a certain interpretation of Genesis is pitted
against almost all of modern science. The creationists are
Christian fundamentalists. They hold every proposition of
scripture to be literally true and to contain authentic—divinely
revealed—scientific and historical knowledge. Thus they insist
that the universe, and all that is in it, began as Genesis appears
to have described it: roughly six to ten thousand years ago, with
its present astronomical structure intact; with its present
species of human, animal, fish, and plant life in the forms that
we now know, going back to the beginning; and with all its
major geological changes to be ascribed to divine intervention—for example (an example the creationist law in Arkansas
cited!), the flood of Noah. In short, they dispute almost every
fundamental theory about nature and its history produced in
the entire spectrum of the contemporary sciences: Big Bang
cosmology, physics, astronomy, and geology, as well as evolutionary biology—though, as is known, they tend wrongly to
blame all of this on Darwin.

Strangely, their leaders are scientists, with doctorates in
science from respectable universities: Berkeley, University of
Pittsburgh, Ohio State, and MIT. And they argue that they can
prove their case "scientifically." This understanding of origins
they term "creation science," to them the only valid science since

it is not based, as for them is the rest of modern science, on atheism. They lost the federal court case in 1981 in Little Rock; the creationist law had stipulated that creation science be given "equal time" with "evolutionary science." in all the schools of Arkansas. We won the case by showing that their "science" was not science at all but religion and thus counter to the First Amendment if taught as science in the schools. Most teachers of science in Arkansas said they would not teach *either one* if forced to give each of them "equal weight." They could, said they, never prove they had given each of these "alternatives" equal emphasis, and thus each science teacher would become continuously vulnerable to prosecution. Thus in effect no science would have been taught in Arkansas had the law gone through.

The creationists have, however, by no means disappeared. In fact, since then they have gained significant power on local school boards, in influence on textbook publishers, and of course in state and national politics via the Christian Coalition. As mentioned above, one leader told me in 1985 that once they take over control of the Republican Party in the nineties, this will be the science taught in public schools. Needless to say, slight changes in the makeup of the Supreme Court might well undo our victory at Little Rock. Then, as a scientific and technological nation, the United States ironically will voluntarily have saddled itself with an educational system designed precisely to subvert science—a strange act of national self-destruction!

The trial was brought against the creationists by the main churches and synagogues of Little Rock: they, not the American Civil Liberties Union, were the initial plaintiffs in the case. In effect, these plaintiffs said: "We are happy to defend science— though we wish they would defend themselves! But we are even more interested in defending our own right to interpret our beliefs as we see fit; and we wish to defend that right against the power and authority of the legislature of Arkansas, which in this law has defined for all of us here the meaning of the doctrine of creation in literalist terms. We believe in creation and so in the meaning of the doctrine in Genesis, but we do not accept their literalist interpretation of either one. The State has in this case ruled for *their* interpretation of our communities' common text. Hence we are bringing this case to court." As is evident, this trial was not about the age and history of the universe, but about the First Amendment, the so-called separation of Church and State. I must say that this latter then disclosed itself to me as a most important amendment, and as they warned, one the Christian Coalition has every intention of reinterpreting and so, in effect, eliminating.

I must also add that for those, like the creationists, who use technology, based as it is on the entire spectrum of modern science, to say they do not accept or believe in science is strange, to me even perverse. A technological culture like ours is established on science: its medicine, its defense, its industry, its entertainment, and so on—it can hardly deny the science it lives on day by day.

Rethinking the Mosaic Account

Our concern, however, will not be with the further development of this controversy, interesting as it is. Rather, we will consider how that controversy has come about. How is it that the main Christian churches and the Reformed and Conservative Jewish communities have come to interpret Genesis in a way compatible with modern science while the creationists have not? What is the difference between a fundamentalist or literalist interpretation of Scripture and a modern or "liberal" one and how did this important difference come about? These are interesting questions, especially because traditionally (before the modern period, say roughly before 1750) both Christian theologians and Jewish scholars (except Spinoza!) interpreted Genesis in a literal as well as in what we would call a "theological" way. They regarded the story of creation in chapters 1 and 2 and of the fall in chapter 3—and the subsequent history—as valid *historical* accounts of how the creation of the universe and of ourselves in it actually happened, as well as containing the religious and theological affirmation of the divine work of creation. As the trial made clear, the leadership of most churches and synagogues and the vast majority of seminaries and biblical scholars do not now regard these chapters as sources for authentic knowledge on scientific questions such as the age of the universe or the processes of its development—nor do they regard its historical accounts as ipso facto authoritative. Rather, they look for the religious and theological meanings of these chapters of Scripture, and, as Gerhard von Rad said, for *their* view of history's sequences, and not for ours, which is obviously different. And our question is: how did this vast change of interpretation come about?

It is my view that the major causes of this shift of hermeneutic—or mode of interpretation—were developments in modern science, especially in geology at the end of the eighteenth and beginning of the nineteenth centuries. Interestingly, Galilean astronomy and Newtonian physics, despite their clear astronomical and cosmological implications, did not particularly disturb the widespread authority of the Mosaic account of origins. Physics and astronomy were then not primarily historical sciences, and many leading scientists in the seventeenth century—in physics, chemistry, and biology—were also Calvinist clergymen who accepted, as did almost everyone else, a literal reading of the Mosaic account. But geology, from its very beginnings in the late eighteenth century, was a *historical* science; it traced the history of the earth. When in the 1790s James Hutton began to uncover the long history of the earth's surface, he said, "I see no signs of a beginning." It was plain at once that six thousand years were not enough and, even more, it was clear that the earth had not always exhibited its present pleasant and habitable rolling hills, gentle valleys, lakes, and oceans. Besides all this, *bones* began to appear: in West Virginia, in Ohio, and then in Russia, bones of species horrifyingly immense and strange, probably extinct,

and hence from a vastly different age; creatures Adam had assuredly not named in Eden, nor Noah ushered into the ark!
Rembrandt Peale and his sons collected some of these bones
and made a fortune exhibiting them to an astounded Europe,
defying anyone, as he said, "to find these creatures on our
present globe. The bones exist; the creatures do not!" Finally,
it is said (by John C. Green) that the thigh bone of a giant
sloth was brought to Jefferson in about 1801; he is reported to
have exclaimed, "What a cow!" and then: "Nature would not
create a species she then allowed to become extinct," showing
he had a very tidy 'eighteenth-century mind and not a messy
nineteenth-century one. Greene adds that Jefferson sent Lewis
and Clark westward in part to find these creatures. It is evident that at this point there was taking place a sea-change, a
paradigm shift, in the understanding of nature's past and of
our past.

It is, therefore, no surprise that theologians—at least
those in close touch with the cultural, and especially the scientific, world of their time—were beginning to rethink how to
understand not only the Mosaic account but also their own
basic religious truths, their doctrines, and even the scriptural
sources of these doctrines—what kind of truths as Christians
they in fact had. Thus in 1825 we find Friedrich Schleiermacher
saying that theology must confine its claims to concepts based
only on the Christian community's experience. For this reason,
religious truth has limits; it does not, he said, communicate information about scientific matters, about historical events, or
even about "philosophical speculations," as he termed them.
What it can articulate on these issues is that we are absolutely
dependent on God as the Absolute Cause of ourselves and of
our world, an experience communicated to us through, not
outside of, our experience of the order of the world's process.
This we know through our experience or consciousness of ourselves. To me, the influence of classical science, as well as of
the new geology, is very evident here.

Most subsequent theology has agreed with this. The theological words or categories have changed a good deal since Schleiermacher's time, but his point about the limits of theology, and the dependence of theology on the community's experience, has not. Now, as then, theology understands itself as being able to witness to God and to God's activity; this witness is based on the community's common experience of God's presence in its history, a presence evident in the events of covenant, and of judgment and of promise as seen by the prophets—and later, for the Christian community, in the events of Jesus' life and death. That presence, or "encounter" as some put it, is received in faith and responded to by witness to others. In turn, that witness, based on the community's experience, has been written down in Scripture. It is a witness to the presence and activity of God, an activity that works through the ongoing order of the world and the strange, even unique, always novel events of history, not outside of them. But, for all theology after Schleiermacher, that witness is also *human*, reflecting, as well as transforming, the thought-forms of its time and of its cultural context—as do preaching and theology themselves. Hence, just as the Hebrew community understood its own life and the history in which it lived as established and preserved by God, the sovereign Lord of history, so correspondingly, they saw the origin of the entire world as also the work of the same God who had rescued, preserved, and loved them. And they understood this deeply religious and important truth in the thought-forms of their time. Thus results the book of Genesis, a tradition of witness lodged in the oral tradition, the poetry and the prose of seventh- and sixth-century Hebrew faith.

Modern theological readings of Genesis—whether in liturgy, devotion, theology, or scholarship—thus look for the religious meanings of each narrative, each command, each psalm—meanings for them ("Hebrew faith") but also for us. They seek for "the word within the words," the religious and moral message there, and not for what Genesis may say about

astronomy, geology, biology, or botany. And as each generation
in Christian and Jewish communities has discovered, that religious and moral message can be as lively, exciting, and healing
as it ever was.

These meanings are expressed through symbols—in
analogies, in metaphors, concepts, or words taken from ordinary experience and now applied to God: the presence of God,
the creative work of God, and the purposes and intentions of
God; power, order, life, love, and care; creation, judgment and
forgiveness, demand and mercy. Thus while the words and narratives of Scripture and of theology—in praise, in celebration,
in repentance and gratitude, and in reflection—refer to what
transcends the human, to God, nonetheless, these words are
human words, part of human language, and so their meanings
are relative to their time and place. Among other things, they
also thus reflect the religious ideas and traditions of the peoples
who preceded the Hebrews and surrounded them. As Arch-
bishop Temple claimed: there are truths of revelation, truths
witnessing to revelation, but there are no revealed truths. This
is the understanding of Genesis that the churches and synagogues of Little Rock wished to defend—an understanding of
which the legislature of Arkansas had not the slightest idea! It
is also the understanding of Genesis that finds itself fully compatible with contemporary science, an important issue for any
religious community that recognizes, uses, celebrates, and con-
tributes to medical science!

The Message of Genesis

What, then, is this message in Genesis, the Word in the words,
and how is it related to us? Saying what this message is could
hardly be a more controversial subject, but allow me to take a
shot at it; after all, I suppose that is why I am writing.

The message of Genesis, at least in the first two chapters,
is that God, the God of the covenant, of the priestly tradition,
and of prophetic faith, has founded or established all things, all

creatures: inorganic, organic, and human. God has, further, set humans here in a habitable and fruitful world to live a meaningful and cooperative life and to multiply; a life of work but also of love, a life in turn under the watchful care of God. Things did not, to be sure, turn out as they were intended to be, as chapters 3 and 4, and the subsequent history, make very clear. Nonetheless, theology, Christian or Jewish, can never speak of human nature as evil or basically evil. The fall, said Augustine, was a *historical* event, and therefore it did not change or destroy the good nature God had given us at creation—as blindness is a disease of the eye and not the nature of the eye, so our nature is warped but not destroyed by sin and hence is redeemable by grace. The fundamental structure of existence is good, replete with immense possibilities, and God is continually filled with mercy for our waywardness. Thus can there be hope for the future. This is the main point: the goodness, care, and mercy of God, and the goodness of the world (despite its ambiguity, pain, and suffering—and mortality) that God has created, is repeated throughout the account. It is thoroughly Hebrew, although many of the images and models through which this is said derive from other traditions that preceded the exodus. It is a unique vision because, I believe, of the uniqueness of the God of the covenant, of the priesthood, and of prophecy—for it was in that relatively later religious context that this text about the beginning was recited and then written.

    This is, we have noted, a text from the ancient world—eighth to fifth centuries B.C.E.—and so reflecting that world in many of its concepts. It is, therefore, a narrative or "myth" strange to us—as the trial in Arkansas clearly revealed. But in important ways it is not *that* strange. And the reason is that, perhaps supremely among the biblical texts, it has formed us and our view of the world in which we live. It has, first of all, provided the most fundamental—"ontological"—presuppositions for the common religious heritage of Judaism and Christianity. All of the central theological concepts and so beliefs of these two traditions assume this view of the world, of ourselves in it, and of our history, namely, as created and preserved by the power, the order, and the love of God, the God of the covenant, of the Torah, and of the prophets. And whatever the secularity of our present in the West (one might well now wish that it were a little *more* secular!), it is clear that these two religious traditions have shaped even our secular existence in many fundamental ways. Western cultural life has had two major sources from the ancient world: Hellenic or classical on the one hand, and Hebraic on the other. Hence many—though not all—of our assumptions about our existence stem from this crucial part of the Hebrew inheritance.

First, and of primary importance, is the theme, repeated in the creation account, that women and men were created in the *image of God.* As a consequence, they are, whatever their race, power, status, gender, or talents, of inestimable value—an aspect of our common tradition that is itself of inestimable value! Though it has taken an excruciatingly long time for the clear implications of these words to work their way fully into our common life, nonetheless these Hebrew words, not Hellenic ones, are the source of what is probably the most creative element in our cultural life: the belief in the equality and the value before God and one another of every human being, or as Kant put it, the value of each person as, like God, an end in themselves.

More surprisingly, our notions of time, and so of history, and hence of the prospects of life in history and in history's communities, are dependent on the interpretation of creation as it is set forth in Genesis. Time itself, said Augustine, interpreting Genesis, is a creation of God; it is a creature like us and thus also under God's power and care. There is, therefore, no Tyche or Fortuna, no blind, remorseless Fate, determining God's purposes, for God is sovereign over all creatures. Accordingly, Augustine continues, there is no Fate determining our existence either, even the least of us. We are all in the hands of God, and of our own freedom—though the latter, as Augustine knew, can get us individually and socially into serious trouble! Hence an impersonal Fate or Destiny, ruling over even the gods, fear of which haunted the late classical world, was banished, and even astrology has been refashioned in this light.

Further, for Genesis, time apparently had a beginning, and it runs its course irreversibly from its beginning at creation to its end in God's promises. Because of the biblical inheritance, therefore, for the world of the West time is linear. It is not cyclical, ever returning upon itself, as it was in Hellenic or classical culture—for the circle, said Aristotle, is the sole way that motion can imitate the perfection of the motionless, or that the changing can mirror the perfection of the changeless. For classical culture, therefore, time was infinite and repeats itself endlessly and meaninglessly. What a contrast to the dynamic and temporally active, and so related, biblical conception of God, and the correlative notion of a linear time filled with unrepeatable and so unique moments, a sequence headed toward its fulfillment under God! Our modern sense of time, secular or religious, is thoroughly dependent on this biblical version of a linear sequence headed toward fulfillment, not on the endless temporal cycles of the classical world. And clearly the Enlightenment and post-Enlightenment—and American!—belief in progress—which is not biblical (recall the fall!)—and the material dialectic of Marxism both have their roots here. They are visions or "myths" of linear, developing time, each seeing history as headed toward its own fulfillment, very different from each other, and very different from their common Hebrew source.

Even more surprisingly, contemporary scientific cosmology has its roots in the Hebrew tradition and so in Scripture. That cosmology sees natural process as a linear temporal sequence, filled with unrepeatable and so unique events, a process extending over immense stretches of time. We are now told it begins with the Big Bang; that it proceeds through the galactic transformations modern astronomy traces; that it issues

further in the deep changes in geological structure and then cul-
minates in those evolutionary mutations in life forms that contemporary biology describes. In many fundamental ways, we are
all—secular as well as religious—children of Genesis who understand our natural world in ways, a variety of ways!—shaped by
this old Hebrew text. For it was precisely *this* contemporary scientific cosmology of development—along with the churches and
synagogues of Little Rock—that was pitted against the creationists. Despite the fact, therefore, that neither the creationists nor
their scientific opponents were aware of this point, each side in
Arkansas was in its own way dependent on Genesis!

Finally, as the Genesis account makes very clear, all of
creation is "good" because it was made by a caring God. Thus
there is, and there can be, nothing essentially evil, an evil, so to
speak, built into things as part of their intrinsic nature, and so
irremovable and unredeemable, a necessary aspect of temporal
and worldly existence. On the contrary, each part of reality has
possibilities for good—even, to Augustine's Hellenistic conster-
nation, matter and the body, both of which, as he had to admit,
God had created and, therefore, despite appearances, must be
good! Again, it has taken a long time for these implications too
to realize themselves. But slowly they have helped to establish
an empirical science of *earthly material* motion (modern science): a new understanding and celebration of the body and its
sensual life, and an inherent confidence that there are always
possibilities of new beginnings latent in almost any historical or
social situation. Changing natural processes, order, spontaneity
and life, novelty, and, especially, our real but relative freedom are
the characteristics of a world created by a caring God. Surprisingly, these form as well the essential structures of our contemporary scientific cosmology. And note, these are aspects as
fundamental to the postmodern vision as they have been to those
of us older dwellers of the twentieth century.

The biblical view, informed by Genesis, is by no
means rosy or overoptimistic. There is, after all, the fall and

its consequences of injustice, conflict, violence, and suffering—and hypocrisy! This true symbol or myth of the fall should have warned us of that which modern culture had ignored but which has been repeatedly validated, namely, that every historical development gives new possibilities for evil as it opens up new opportunities for good. Nonetheless, it remains the case that the goodness of creation in its essential nature—in its inherent possibilities—means that there is always in history, whatever the grim actualities of our present, the chance for renewal, for new beginnings. And I must say, in the light of daily reports of near insanity in so many of the world's capitals, I am very glad that this confidence and hope retain their strength in our common life.

God and Human Beings

A couple of further points may be appropriate at the close of these remarks. First of all, I repeat that this interpretation of the first two chapters—which stems from the theology of the early and middle parts of the last century, and which I can certainly not disavow!—has been very much debated, and controverted, since. To me it represents the heart of the long traditional influence of these chapters of Genesis on the religious self-understanding of the Christian and Jewish communities and on our wider cultural life. Nonetheless, it remains only one of many present scholarly readings. As my esteemed New Testament colleague Norman Perrin once said to me on another issue: "Which one of my fifty-seven Christologies in the New Testament do you wish to use this week in your theology, Langdon?"

It is, moreover, appropriate to mention two places where this interpretation from the 1930s, 1940s, and 1950s seems now to be really lacking, though considering the relativity of all things historical, certainly theology and biblical studies, this is hardly surprising. First of all, while it can be said that an earlier generation believed firmly in equality, nonetheless the rise of gender consciousness since the 1960s has made all of us much more aware than before of the tone of male dominance that seems to permeate these accounts of our creation, and certainly most subsequent theological and scholarly interpretations of them. Surprisingly, to me, this imbalance is worse in the Yahwist account of chapter 2 (where Eve is created out of Adam's rib or side) than in the later Priestly account of chapter 1, where God creates male and female at the same time. One can, I believe, claim legitimately that all of the movements of liberation since the 1950s and 1960s represent long-term effects of the imago dei, but there is at the same time little doubt that the accounts themselves—the rib, the role of help-meet, and so on—have (as the Southern Baptists have so elegantly manifested to us) been a large part of the problem of the subordination of women as well as the ultimate source of the answer.

Second, there is the status of nature, also a matter of a new and sharper consciousness on the part of all of us, a consciousness, let us recall, that has been with us only since the late 1960s and the early 1970s. I do not think it fair to blame all our exploitation of and indifference to nature on our biblical heritage, as does Lynn White. A humanist culture also centers its values on human beings and their needs, as John Dewey showed. Arguably, moreover, the scientific viewpoint tends to objectify its every object, and hence it also objectifies (makes mere manipulable objects out of) the natural processes that science studies. Thus science, as well as Christian desacralization, has helped to strip nature of its intrinsic value. And surely, the development of technological power has only increased these tendencies. In modern technological culture the age-old human domination of nature has threatened to become extravagantly exploitative, capable in the end of destroying the fertility of the earth, and so in fact "demonic." Hence, technology has provided effective instruments for the infinite and ruthless greed— what Buddhists term *desire*—which has driven modern life even more relentlessly than it did ancient life. Perhaps this is what a wise Genesis meant in speaking of human wrongdoings as corrupting and polluting the earth.

Still, with these necessary caveats, let me say that a close and aware rereading of these chapters shows that the critique of the biblical tradition on ecological grounds, that it is has ignored the value and integrity of nature, is well-taken indeed. Incidentally, I repeated the following critique of this inheritance at an ecological conference some years ago on the same platform with Carl Sagan. After my talk, he shook my hand warmly and said—he was a very charming man—"I'm so glad to hear someone from religion criticizing religion!" I thanked him and said I would be equally glad to hear someone from science criticizing science. He said "Humph!" and walked away.

But to get back to my theme. The whole of Scripture, not least our two chapters, is centered to be sure on God and God's doings; nonetheless, like the First and the Second Commandments, it is also centered on the human, on the relation of God to women and men, and on the relations of men and women to one another. In that sense it is, while dramatically theistic, also humanist—it reveres and so dignifies the human. And we have noted the very great benefits accruing from that emphasis on the value of the human. There is, however, always a shadow side to all good things on earth, including religion, and even— though more surprising—including humanism! This is a side that has also become plain to us in our generation: that nature is here strikingly ignored if not demeaned. Barth was right when he said (with approval) that nature is in Scripture essentially a backdrop or, better, the mere *stage* on which the drama between God and human beings (he said "men") is played out. Although Barth was right in this general assessment, there are wonderful passages in the psalms and in Job, especially, where nature is portrayed—shall I say?—as also made in the image of God. And by that I mean that nature is celebrated as manifesting God's power and order as well as God's care, where the infinity and immensity of God are disclosed to us, and so where

God's glory is plainly set forth. Still, these are, let us admit, subordinate themes.

Above all, that repeated divine injunction or, better, command to exercise dominion over nature and over nature's creatures, in fact to subdue them, clearly spells out the subordination of nature to our human interests in ways that offend our contemporary convictions. Of course, we must recall with some empathy that ancient cultures were then themselves just moving out of their own religious, moral, and social self-understanding as *subordinate* to nature's patterns and powers. They were becoming at this point for the first time conscious of the human as unique and so of the social community as markedly different from the natural processes around them. One finds this clearly set forth in the distinction between nature and art, nature and polis, in Greek thought, as it is clearly also there, as we have just noted, in Hebrew understanding. At this point, one might say, humans could only barely and precariously secure their own existence over against nature's gigantic threats to everything on which they depended.

Because of technology and industrialism, and ultimately because of science, however, we now know of no such precarious existence day by day with regard to nature; rather, it is *history* that terrifies us. We have subdued nature and established almost total human dominion over it. Only once in a while does nature surprise us and dominate us. This dominion over nature has, let us note, been the aim of humans since the beginning, and explicitly since Francis Bacon spoke of knowledge as power, the power to effect what we want. And, like all apparently good things, this new dominion through knowledge has now revealed itself as also a vast potentiality for destruction: destruction of nature and, as a consequence, destruction of ourselves. Nature has now come under the dominion of history, of *our* wills, and so the dominion of the waywardness as well as of the creativity of human freedom, a terrifying transition indeed! Hence we now read these chapters differently than we did in the 1950s. In modern existence, dominion over nature has in truth become the subjection, exploitation, and destruction of nature by our intentions, by our freedom; it is an example, therefore, of human sin—of inordinate greed and pride, and thus it is a fit occasion for repentance and for reform.

In sum, to me an even deeper amendment of these chapters is essential. God has, to be sure, created women and men in the divine image. But also, if we take the psalms and Job seriously, God has created *nature* also as an image or mirror of God: a mirror of God's mystery, power, order, and life. Creation means, therefore, not only the infinite glory of God and the goodness of life but also the intrinsic value of nature. Above all, nature and nature's processes are a mirror of the divine union of life with death, that is, of the power, everywhere patterned in natural process, with which God brings new life constantly out of death. This praise of nature as God's creation in God's image might have been said, but was not, in the first two chapters. Let us proceed to say it now.

Part 2

Theology's Struggle
with Modernity

6

reinhold niebuhr

If one had asked in the 1930s, 1940s, and 1950s who was the best known and most respected theologian in America, the answer would certainly have been Reinhold Niebuhr, of Union Seminary in New York. In the middle of the 1950s, he suffered a serious stroke, and inevitably his influence waned—and, incidentally, it was then that his friend and colleague Paul Tillich became the leading theological voice. Both of them had a very wide influence on American culture. In fact, in those years, they were the leading reflective figures (philosophy had, so to say, opted out of cultural affairs)—Tillich in art, psychotherapy, and philosophy; Niebuhr in political theory, ethics, and social affairs. Each, especially Niebuhr, had enthusiastic secular followers, most of whom sought unsuccessfully, I think, to appropriate the obvious wisdom of these theologians without their essential religious dimension.

The reason for Niebuhr's secular prominence was his brilliance as a social and political analyst; he was also a very influential political activist. He established and edited *Christianity and Society*, a liberal journal, and in 1946 he founded the ADA (Americans for Democrative Action), a liberal yet noncommunist group that was very important politically for the next twenty-five years. I began my theological studies as a student of these two transcendent figures in both our theological and our cultural lives. Most of us expected that this wide and important cultural role—in art or in politics—was perfectly possible for a good theologian. Little did we realize (until later, when *we* tried it) how exceedingly rare it was!

Niebuhr became prominent in the early 1930s, with the publication in 1933 of *Moral Man and Immoral Society* and in 1934 of *Reflections on the End of an Era*. These were books largely of political analysis with hardly any theological content. Nevertheless, they had an amazing impact in American social thought and on liberal religion. I can recall in 1932—I was thirteen—my father coming out of his office waving a copy of *Moral Man and Immoral Society* and saying "Reinnie's gone crazy!"—and most liberal social gospel ministers like my father felt the same way, though by the end of the decade they came to agree with him. Why did these books have such a profound and disturbing impact?

Realism and Optimism

Most of liberal culture in America—secular, academic, and religious alike—was deeply optimistic about society and about history. Like Europeans before World War I, liberals believed thoroughly in historical progress. As science, technology, and industry have developed or evolved, so correspondingly have legal, political, and social institutions—from autocratic and despotic governments to democracy, from racial and religious intolerance to tolerance, from authoritarian and dogmatic religion to liberal, congregational religion. Social customs and laws alike were surely getting better, evolving, as species have evolved, into higher forms. Accordingly, people were becoming more moral, society was becoming Christian, and the task of the churches was building the kingdom here on earth. I was brought up in this sort of faith, and it was this faith that Niebuhr challenged in these books. Barth had done just this in Europe in 1918 after World War I; Niebuhr did it in the early thirties in America. His, however, was not by appeal to the

Bible, though that came later, but by empirical argument, by pointing to the actual character of contemporary capitalistic, racial, and international life. If you read these books, you will see that he proved his case as, of course, was the entire course of history to do a decade later!

And what was it he was saying in these volumes? He did not deny that institutions and even moral customs and laws had progressed; later he was to formulate this more clearly. But within these new modes of social relations—modern nation-states, democratic politics, and especially the commercial relations of capitalistic society, self-concern or self-interest, the grasping for power, wealth, status, security—remained as predominant as ever. And this "natural impulse," as he then called it, creates now as in the past the same devastating suffering for those who are its victims. In a social struggle, classes may say they are acting for universal values: the owners for order and stability, the workers and underprivileged for justice. But in fact each is acting for power and wealth, the one to preserve them, the other to gain them. Nations claim to struggle for justice and peace, but in fact even the "peace-loving nations" (as we called ourselves in World War II) were acting from their own self-interests. For this reason, Niebuhr insisted that no group will ever be dislodged from power solely by persuasion, by arguments, however academically elegant: "Reason is the servant of impulse before it is its master!" Thus only a power opposed to ruling groups, challenging them, and even forcing them—a political, economic, or, in the last resort, military power—will dislodge them and create a more just situation. Clearly justice is on the side of those with less power and less wealth, but the justice of the latter's cause does not, said Niebuhr, imply their greater virtue. When they (for example, the proletariat) gain power, they may well dominate as did once the nobility and now the bourgeoisie—and Russia's communism showed he was right.

The second main point was that there is a notable difference between the moral behavior of individuals—where there is

some real possibility of self-sacrifice for others, though it is rare
enough—and the behavior of communities: families, clans,
classes, races, genders, states, or nations. With the latter, the
self-interest of the group is invariably the predominant factor.
And many things that individuals will not do, a group will do
to further its fortunes and, of course, those of its members. It is
perfectly possible for the same persons to act quite morally or
"respectably," according to the customs of their society and
yet, in relation to persons in other groups, and particularly to
other groups, to act very unethically. Hence there can be,
without contradiction, the pious slave owner, the respectable
member of a ruling class or aggressive nation, the "moral"
member of an oppressive race. In these cases, while all are apparently moral as individuals, nonetheless they can join with
others of their group and act with exceeding self-concern and
devastating destruction.

Patriotism, says Niebuhr, is particularly enlightening
on this point. The patriotic individual sacrifices himself or
herself for the group and is thus for all of us one of the highest symbols of morality. It is this sacrifice of person for group
that most social scientists call "altruism." But the action that
the group does through the moral loyalty of the patriot may
well be very immoral, in fact evil, as in an aggressive war. It
is for this strange reason that the very highest level of the
moral *real* altruism may be the *challenge* of what the group
does, and ultimately the self-sacrifice of the individual in *op-
posing* the morality of the group, as in the rare but illuminating cases of Socrates and Jesus. In any case, Niebuhr insists
that because in the relatively stable historical situation of
modern life, individuals act with seeming morality. This does
not mean that as members of social groups—in class, racial,
economic, or political matters—they in any way escape doing
and supporting injustice. Group relations in our age remain
as self-interested and often as brutal as in the less "moral"
days of the past.

The final point of these books was even more shocking to secular and religious optimists. Niebuhr's point was that reason—scientific, economic, and political intelligence—and religion (even liberal religion) were as ambiguous as the rest of culture. For the secular and academic communities, reason—especially scientific and empirical reason—represented the sole principle of objectivity and impartiality in human affairs. Here, in principle, prejudice and self-interest were eliminated, and hence an informed intelligence, as John Dewey said, is the sole means of salvation in social life. Correspondingly, religious liberals agreed that while dogmatic and authoritarian religion had done much harm in the past, nonetheless a nondogmatic religion, tolerant of other points of view and committed to social justice, could also provide a basis for salvation in social history.

Niebuhr did not deny either point. But, he said, such objectivity in a *social crisis*, as opposed to a lab or a Sunday school, is a rare and a moral achievement. Both reason and religion can and frequently have provided justification for group selfishness even more than they have provided challenges to it. The union of science and the military in all recent history, in World War II and in the more current India–Pakistan relations, shows the first point, and the almost universal support of their nations by the religious groups of the twentieth century shows the second. I might add that on this same point, the churches of Japan, Germany, England, and the United States have had a better record challenging the evils of the State than have the academic faculties, the scientific laboratories, or the educational administrations in the same communities.

These affirmations, therefore, represented the main points of Niebuhr's early political work. As is evident, there is little theology here and even less reference to the biblical view. In fact, his interpretations of these insights retained most of the older liberal assumptions. Although, therefore, these insights were fascinating, one could not help but wonder what sort of theological perspective was implied in them. This theological perspective began to appear at the end of the decade. First came *Beyond Tragedy* in 1936, a series of sermons setting these insights into a semi-neoorthodox interpretation of the Bible. Niebuhr had begun to discover the biblical and theological grounds for his empirical analysis of social affairs. Then, of course, in 1939–40 came volume 1 on *The Nature and Destiny of Man*, and in 1943 volume 2. Here the developed theology congruent with these insights, what Niebuhr called "biblical faith" or the "biblical view," was elaborated. The rest of my remarks will be devoted to describing in part that theological viewpoint with which he is identified.

The Human Spirit

Despite Niebuhr's well-known emphasis on the reality and the universality of sin, he nonetheless thoroughly believed in the creativity, intellectual power, and moral possibilities of the human spirit—what made each human unique and of value, history full of novel creations and events, and community a locus of justice and love. Because of human creativity, history is thus constantly changing and is full of indeterminate possibilities for development. In this sense, Niebuhr was a child of modern culture, with its emphasis on historical process, on dynamic change, and on constant development. This creative spiritual power Niebuhr identified as the imago dei, the image of God in human beings. And he described it as the capacity for self-transcendence: the essential ability of each human being to look at herself, to recall the past and project into the future, to see far outward into space and even up to infinity. Humans can thus transcend themselves, their time and space and the structure of nature and of world around them. This is the seat of imagination, reason, and judgment, and of moral possibility. For humans are free in their spirits of their particular *spatio* (temporal locus), and thus are they capable of the new and are thereby forced to decide in part their path in each next moment.

The human spirit thus towers over all that is earthly; it reaches toward God and, as Augustine said, realizes itself truly only in God. Nonetheless, this self-transcendence is, says Niebuhr, creaturely and not divine. It never loses its finite seat in a particular self, community, culture, nationality, race, or gender. However lofty its imaginations, thoughts, and projects, these latter reflect that particular locus. The spirit is capable of the universal, of transcending its time, place, and culture, but it always shares the particular and finite perspective of its origin. My theology remains basically American, male, white, twentieth century—and I had best remember this.

To express this ineradicable finitude and particularity of each human, Niebuhr uses another biblical category: the *creatureliness* of all life, including human life. Thus each creature is born and dies, appears in a particular temporal and spatial context, is dependent on all else around him (on family, community, and world alike), and remains dependent and mortal throughout its life, whatever heights his political, artistic, intellectual, or moral accomplishments may reach. We note that death, mortality, is for Niebuhr, as for most of his theological contemporaries, a part of the God-given creatureliness of women and men, not the result of sin. It is an aspect of a *good* creation, of the goodness of natural life, whose dependencies, like its creativity, we share. Thus, like all other life, human existence is vulnerable and brief, with the continual possibility of suffering. However, says Niebuhr, with faith and hope for the future in God's providence, these contingencies can be surmounted in courage and creative action.

We therefore are and remain creatures. Relativity and finitude, embodying only one perspective among many, thus infect all human creations: thought, imagination, morals, and religion alike. Each remains creaturely and not divine. There is no way, therefore, that reason can attain the universality it seeks and often claims, or the moral will the objective judgment of which it so frequently boasts. On the contrary, each will approach universality only in so far as each is willing to recognize the partial character of all it represents. Despite the infinite creativity of the human spirit, there are no ultimates in history, secular or religious. This emphasis on relativity and finitude is, we note, also thoroughly modern, as was the emphasis on creativity and development. Niebuhr postulated these characteristic assumptions of modernity and always argued, with some justice, that ultimately both were biblical and dependent finally on a biblical faith.

It is, continues Niebuhr, out of this situation given us by our Creator—of finiteness and creatureliness on the one hand and of self-transcendence on the other, or necessity and freedom (as he puts it)—that both the creativity and the sin of humans arise. Let us consider Niebuhr's analysis of sin, for which he is best known. As creaturely, humans are like all life dependent and vulnerable: dependent on their natural environment, on other persons and groups, and on the ongoing events of the history in which they live. They can prosper through their creative ingenuity, but they can also die, as does all life— and ultimately they will. But, being self-transcendent, knowing the past and foreseeing the future, humans know this: alone they know that they are mortal, that there is an enemy over the next hill, a rival next door at the office, the risk of want for next winter. Thus they are anxious. In their freedom, their freedom is disturbed, their spirits troubled. Hence they seek to secure themselves against these threats. They make themselves the center of their world, as if they were that center. In biblical language, they replace God with themselves, they take the place of God. And in the process, they are violent, cruel, and destructive toward others. Self-centeredness breeds injustice, and the cycle of sin, violence, and destruction begins.

There is no necessity here. In principle this creaturely anxiety, fed by spirit, can be resolved by spirit, by faith in God's providence and care. Thus we are each responsible, and we know that we are responsible. The inevitable consequence in each of us of the uneasy conscience, of guilt, following on self-centeredness and injustice, shows the central role of freedom in all of our sin. The earliest of religions, the latest pop novel, not to mention every courtroom, reveal this universal presence of the awareness, yes *knowledge*, of responsibility or guilt, and of the participation of freedom in all of our dealings with one another.

We are anxious, however, not only about security and power—for we are also intellectual, moral, and religious beings. We seek after truth, but our truth is partial, creaturely. We are uneasily aware of this, too, and of the radical void with which this faces us. We therefore claim our own truth to be ultimate. We make moral judgments, and we must; but they too are relative, reflective of our own partial customs and traditions. Hence again, anxious about our moral status, we claim our moral judgments to be ultimate, in effect God's judgments. Incidentally, such judgments always declare us to be righteous and our opponents wrong, as every international altercation shows. Finally, the most serious sin of all, we claim our spirits to represent the divine, our religion to be God's religion. The ultimate sin is to claim to be God, and this pride religion has illustrated throughout history. True religion, therefore, facing the divine transcendence, knows first of all its own partiality and guilt, and repents. Without an initial repentance in the encounter with the divine judgment, religious commitment becomes the acme of spiritual pride. Niebuhr calls all these claims of ultimacy *pride*, the pride of the creature taking the place of its Creator. Pride defies God and results at once in injustice. Here for Niebuhr is the true source of history's tragedy, suffering, and despair. And despite the evident development of institutions, legal codes, and moral norms in history, this sin in all its forms of power, intelligence, morals, and religion remains as a most significant dynamic force in history, the major cause of injustice.

As he had said at the start of his career, it was only an unusual individual who could feel her power or her wisdom to be such that she could claim to be the center of the world. Hence most of us make this claim *together*, through the community of which we are a part: a tribe, family, nation, race, gender, profession, church. Serious sins are mostly communal sins. We make the interests of our relevant group central, and we give ourselves to our group, to its security and success, with all our loyalty and power. Thus result the social, the group, sins of historical life: sins of class, of nation, of race, of gender. These communities support, defend, and secure the individuals within them—as the social power of men over women aids each man in *his* domination of women. Thus the pride of communities, given religious sanction in the past and moral sanction in our present, represents the major form of sin in history. It is thus that people who are individually good can, as we saw, unconsciously sin through the pride and cruelty of their community. And in each small community and home, as well as in the largest groups, the same pride can show itself and the same injustice result.

One final point, no individual or community can face squarely the fact that they do make themselves the center of their universe. This is too devastating for any of us to admit. Hence, says Niebuhr, we deceive ourselves that what we do is right and that it is our moral and religious obligation. Nations go to war mainly for self-interest. And though that be the fundamental or ground, they will argue that they are defending God, their sacred tradition, peace, order, and democracy. They claim that what they do for themselves they are really doing for "values." This self-deception makes it very difficult for people, and especially for communities, to admit their fault. If they do, they seem to be denying all that is of value in their tradition or religion. To confess is thus the height of spiritual self-transcendence, transcendence even over one's own self-interest and guilt. As Niebuhr put it, the final paradox is that we are most free when we admit our unfreedom, our sin, and repent inwardly.

To Niebuhr, the myth of the fall expresses or discloses this situation of ourselves and of all other humans: in each the fault of all, in all the fault of each, as Friedrich Schleiermacher put it. This myth—and Niebuhr was one of the first to use the word *myth* in this context—is thus *true*, but it is not *literally* true. It points to a true dimension or aspect of all of our lives, not to an actual historical event. It thus discloses, but does not explain, our situation. Like the symbol of the good creation or that of the image of God, the symbol of original sin provides the most fundamental framework for our self-understanding. None of them, any more than the symbols relevant to God, can be taken literally. But this gives us the basis for understanding ourselves as creatures made in the image of God and yet haunted by a universal sinfulness—which is assuredly the way we actually are.

History's Meaning

"Where there is history, there is freedom; where there is freedom, there is sin." These are, as we have seen, the fundamental elements of Niebuhr's understanding of men and women, and so of history. History is, therefore, dynamic, creative, and indeterminately progressive in its forms of cultural and political, moral and intellectual, life. But within these developments, self-concern and self-deception lurk continuously, as every daily news report shows. Niebuhr, however, never despaired of history's meaning. That meaning was not because of human moral progress or because of the gradual victory of good over evil, as the optimistic culture of the West had held. Rather it was because of God, God's power, God's righteousness, and above all, God's mercy. Despite his evident realism, Niebuhr never questioned that history had a meaning, nor that God's reality and purposes, God's sovereignty, were the sole grounds for that meaning. He never doubted the reality of divine grace, nor the sovereign rule of God over history and what transcends history—and so the final victory of grace.

It is impossible to go into this side—the grace side—of Niebuhr's thought now, though it is important in understanding him. Here Niebuhr speaks from faith, from what he called "biblical" faith, since here—especially with regard to eschatology, final judgment, and final redemption—he could not, as in all else before, also appeal to experience. It was, for him, through God alone that history maintained and would, at the end, disclose a final meaning, but that promise of meaning has been disclosed beforehand to Israel and especially in Jesus Christ.

Since all humans, and all of us, are sinners—though not equally so—this meaning is not represented by the victory of the good over the evil—for there *are* no righteous—but the final mercy of God, which accepts those who are sinners when they turn from their sin and repent. Here the disclosure in the Christ, especially of the atoning love shown in the cross, is for Niebuhr crucial for understanding the final redemptive meaning of the historical life of each of us, and of history itself— which remains to the end ambiguous. Through that event, as interpreted in Scripture, we are certain of God's mercy, even to each of us. Thus are we assured of God's power and love, which together can justify our wayward existence, fulfill and complete the fragmentary character of our life history, and in the end bring us into God's eternal love. Niebuhr said it was not wise for any theologian to know too much about the temperature of hell or the furniture of heaven. But about the everlasting love and mercy of God, this we know well in the prophets and in Jesus Christ.

7

an introduction to tillich

Paul Tillich is a strange theologian for us to absorb and understand. He is a philosopher with a complex, coherent theological system; at the same time, he is an existentialist with a deeply personal reference to all he says. As a woman said after one of his lectures in Nashville: "I did not understand a word that professor was saying, but he was talking about me every minute." I shall here try to show how these two elements—ontological philosophy and personal, existential reference—fit well together.

We should also recall that Tillich was a founding member of the Religious Socialist movement in Germany in the late 1920s, and that he was removed from his professorship in 1933 both for that fact and for his protest against the exclusion of the Jews from the universities by the newly ruling Nazis. Moreover, in the 1950s, after he had been in the United States for twenty years—at Union and then at Harvard—he was asked to be the central speaker at the fiftieth anniversary of the Museum of Modern Art in New York and to address the American Psychoanalytic Society at one of its yearly meetings. His is, therefore, a multifaceted, multidimensional thought. I shall try to introduce us to what are, for me, the most intriguing, yet strange, aspects of his theological reflection. For beginning reading, I recommend some of his sermons (for example, *The Shaking of the Foundations*) and that little classic *The Courage to Be*.

The first aspect of Tillich's theology that strikes us as strange is that Tillich presents us with a philosophy; his theology is *ontological*, and ontology is reflection on the structure of being. What has this to do with religion? we ask. Religion concerns my personal soul in relation to a personal God, and at best my morality. What has this to do with the impersonal category of being? The first answer, probably, is that Tillich was born a philosopher and could not help it. But more interesting are the following:

1. Tillich felt (and he was right) that our ordinary understanding was plagued by a dualism that penetrates our whole existence: the dualism between objective bodies and inner spirits, between a determined world of atoms and a personal world of persons, a dualism that has dominated the West since Galileo and Newton. To Tillich, both of these are abstractions from the experienced unity of life. In each moment, we experience the unity of our bodies and our purposes, in moving our arms or speaking, not to mention our bruised shins and our inner "ouch." Thus we need a category that includes both, for being includes both the objects of our experience and the inner spirit that monitors and directs that experience. And, as Tillich will show us, religion especially has to do with much more than the moral life and the status of our soul.

2. There is—and it is related to the above—the obvious disunity of our cultural life. In academia, this is represented by the gulf between the humanities as the study of the creative human spirit and the sciences as the study of impersonal nature. In class, Tillich one time characteristically addressed this point: "I go to the mall and I buy food for my body; I stop by my lawyer to write my will; I go to the doctor for my liver; then I spend some time in a gallery for my soul; I stop by my shrink for my wounded psyche; and then I have a chocolate sundae. *I* do all this, but these areas are for us totally unrelated, and faculty in them cannot talk together (faculty can only talk together at

the bar, and then about football)." Again, he insisted, to express
this unity evident in all cultural life, a category is needed that
includes and unites the outer and the inner, the objective body
and the subjective spirit—and this category is *being*, in which
both share.

3. Religion, said Tillich, is much more than the moral
state of the soul, important as that is for religion. It includes
health, many aspects of anxiety and fear that are not immediately moral, and, of course, the issues of the meaning of life
and of death. Religion concerns *all* of our existence, each of
its aspects, at the depth of our being. Religion is, said Tillich,
ultimate concern, that which is absolutely prior for us, and
that includes everything that concerns our being and our nonbeing, what most fundamentally threatens us and most fundamentally rescues us. Thus in order to understand religion
(theology), we must understand the structure of our being, as
to understand health and disease necessitates an understanding of the structure of our bodies—though you do not have to
know all that in order to get sick! Again, the structure of our
being and knowledge of its essential nature are fundamental
for understanding religion.

Being thus refers both to the objects of our world and to
ourselves among those objects, to world and to self. And understanding being means understanding the essential structure
of each. This includes objects and so, of course, science. But
science requires a mind directed by logic, and it requires inner
purposes directed toward the truth. Science necessitates both
the objective and the subjective. Being, said Tillich, is most directly understood and known from the inside in self-awareness
(Kierkegaard and Heidegger), for humans are present to
themselves in self-awareness. We can know much about a tree,
Tillich once said, but only from the outside; we do not know
what it is to be a tree. But this we do know as humans; here we
understand being from within. Hence: "Man is the entrance

into being." Thus, being in Tillich's ontology is not at all impersonal but begins with personal awareness; being here is
neither dualistic nor objective.

Religion and Culture

Tillich is a philosopher and so he believes in reason—not always true of a theologian! Reason for Tillich is the "culture
creating power of the human spirit." Thus it is not as in our ordinary speech merely science and logic, analysis and principles
of management; reason is also creative of imagination and also
of art, literature, politics, economics, morals, and religion. As
aspects of culture, all are the creative works of reason. Thus the
split in culture we spoke of between science and the humanities
is not one between reason and imagination, reason and emotion, reason and ends; it is a split *in* reason, a breakup of reason, and so it is fatal. Reason without emotion and ends is
technical reason only; technical reason unguided by values
quickly becomes *controlling reason*—a reason purportedly
on its own and neutral, but one actually guided by hidden
ends: greed, dominance, and desire. It is reason split off from
self-control—moral control—separated from concern for worth.

Reason also, said Tillich, has a ground, an infinite, creative, and uniting ground. This divine ground provides the
necessary bases or presuppositions for thinking and for cultural
creativity. In this ground, we experience the unity of object and
subject, of reality and logic, of reality and inquiry. Tillich
names these objective and subjective *logos*. There can be no inquiry or science without this presupposition of unity, which
makes thinking relevant to the reality it thinks about. Also
there can be no inquiry or science without an ultimate concern
for truth. Cheating disposes of science as corrupt courts dispose
of justice. In both cases, the institutions of culture—science and
law—depend directly on ultimate concerns, on a commitment
to integrity, to truth, and to justice, however wayward our
practice may be.

These presuppositions, these ultimate concerns for truth, value, and worth, lie back of all of culture and of each culture. No creative community life is possible without a deep sense of the meaning and worth of participation in the vocations of that community. This sense of ultimate meaning that must permeate a culture's life represents for Tillich the *religious substance* of the culture. This is, in short, the culture's vision of the real and of its relation to our own being, that is to say, to truth and knowledge, to the ends and worth of life, a sense of truth, beauty, and justice (Tillich always thought of himself as a Platonist). Each creative culture has such a unique religious substance that characterizes and is expressed through its art, literature, science, politics, economics, morals, and religion. In this sense, each creative culture is *theonomous:* grounded in the ultimate and unconditioned (in ultimate concern) and yet autonomously and freely creative through all the powers of human being. In Tillich, the relation to God and the freedom of human creativity go together, and they disappear together.

Tillich says that when this religious depth to the culture— its sense of ultimate reality, meaning, and value—recedes, then a deep void, a void of anxiety or emptiness, appears. The religious substance of the culture, whether that culture be ancient or modern, is expressed in the categories of myth, and it is, said Tillich, enacted in the cults of the culture. When the mythical base of the culture becomes absurd to, and rejected and ignored by, the culture itself, then the autonomous culture itself loses its meaning. And into that void there rushes a new religious *heteronomy,* the sacred as oppressive. Fanaticism is the anxious reaction to an eroded autonomy, an uncontrolled relativity and meaninglessness, a religious vacuum, and every culture is vulnerable to it. For Tillich, the dream of a thoroughly secular culture based on autonomous reason alone is an illusion. In the anxious void of relativity, the absolute will reappear as ideology, as heteronomy; religion becomes the basis of repression and not of freedom. We shall speak of this process again.

Being and Nonbeing

For Tillich, the main task of philosophy is to describe the structure of finite being. This description is not just one of objects,
as in science. Rather, it must include all of reality, and hence
also the subject, for example, the scientist. Ontology embraces
both outer and inner, both objective and subjective, since all
experience and knowing presupposes both. This task is necessary for culture, of course, lest a society live with quite unex-
amined presuppositions and assumptions. However, it is also
necessary for religion and for reflection on religion, namely,
theology.

Religion, says, Tillich, is *ultimate concern:* whatever is
absolutely prior for us, whatever concerns us ultimately, that is
our "god" and to it we devote all our powers and energy. Thus
religion—though it may well be misguided in its worship—if
genuine, concerns our being and our nonbeing, the ultimate issues of our existence. Hence, to understand religion, we must
understand the structure of our being and what concerns us ultimately. In this way, philosophy undergirds the understanding
of religion, which is theology, by uncovering the structure of
our being.

That structure at its most fundamental level is one of finite being or, as Tillich intriguingly put it, "being bounded by
non-being." We are, and yet we are contingent (we need not
be); we are aware of this, and so we are free. We are "finite
freedom." We can see this strange combination of being, contingency, and spontaneity in all entities through scientific inquiry (atoms, mountains, animals). But as humans we know
this most directly from the inside, much more immediately
than from the outside. Again, as Tillich put it, "Man is the entrance into being." In us, being is illuminated, self-aware, as
Heidegger, following Kierkegaard, had said.

Now to return to Tillich, finitude known from the inside
is *anxiety*—anxiety because our being is contingent, that is,
bounded and threatened by nonbeing. It is, and yet it may not

be; it is contingent, and of this we are inwardly aware. This anxiety suffuses us up and down the scale of our whole being; anxiety about security, about place, about status, about wealth, about the future, about the meaning of our life, about our guilt or innocence, about our death. Anxiety is our continual and pervasive companion. It is part of our essential being; it is not sin, but it is the effective condition of sin—its threshold, so to speak.

The answer to this universal situation of anxiety is *courage*, the courage to face our finitude and its limitations, our relativity and our radical insecurity, and our ultimate death. Only with courage can we be creative and not frantically destructive in our life. Courage is the ground of the possibility of meaning and hence finally of culture itself. And only the ultimate and unconditioned, the ground of our being and not some other being, can be the source of courage. All finite gods, for Tillich, are too much like us—contingent, anxious, and insecure. They, too, are threatened by nonbeing, and so, again like us, they are dependent on some ultimate beyond themselves, as in classical culture the finite gods were dependent upon Fate or Tyche. Only the ultimate and unconditional, therefore, is God, the ground and source of our finitude and the source of our courage to be. We note that in Tillich, the unconditional God (and for that reason) is also the ground of our autonomy and freedom, both of which require the courage to be. This is, as we noted, *theonomy:* a deep relation to the ground that makes possible our autonomy. It is contrasted with *autonomy,* our freedom and self-direction without the ground, and with *heteronomy,* the return of the sacred against autonomy and so as oppressive.

This courage is universal, limited by no particular faith or cultural situation, as the relation to the ground is universal. But without it, life and creative life are impossible. Without it, we will do anything to get our lost security back. This is the estrangement or sin, a fascinating issue in Tillich but one we shall not cover here. Each culture begins with a theonomous vision, a vision of the union of the ultimately real, the sacred, and the good. Tillich's favorite example was the vision of the identity of nature and reason that dominated the modern Enlightenment. Inspired by the glowing excitement of modern science, this was a vision that gradually saw itself as independent of the transcendent and that slowly separated itself off from its sacred ground—the ground that provided the very unity of objective and subjective, nature and reason, that formed the original essence of the modern vision. Hence this vision began to be suffused with a sense of relativity, skepticism, and meaninglessness, and it became subject to the appearance of a new heteronomy.

This analysis of the development of modern culture from an original theonomy through autonomy to a new and lethal heteronomy was certainly validated for Tillich by the experience of Germany. Germany was, let us recall, the center of modern science and of liberal culture, but it was overcome by a radically oppressive theology, built on demonic, distorted but sacred elements: blood, soil, and *Volk*. It is also very relevant and sobering for us to remember this in our present battles, in the very midst of our technical and scientific supremacy, with a similarly heteronomous fundamentalism.

Time and Space

Let me conclude with a small segment of Tillich's analysis of finitude and its ground, a segment that is, I think, vintage Tillich. As we have noted, Tillich begins by outlining philosophically the structure of finite being. In this enterprise, he embarks on the search for basic categories, a search that has characterized the entire history of philosophy. Among the elements Tillich uncovers are what he terms the *categories*, the inescapable forms of our thought and speech about everything, and hence—so we believe—the forms that objectively characterize all that is (note the immense presupposition of the unity of objective and subjective here!). They are time, space, causality, and substance. What these entail has been endlessly debated since Aristotle.

Tillich is, however, fundamentally a theologian, and that is nowhere more apparent than in this connection. That is to say, he is concerned with these universal and essential structures only as bearers of the existential problematic of our contingent finitude, as sources of anxiety on the one hand and of courage on the other, as grounds of our *religious* existence. Incidentally, it is, I think, a bit of a surprise to most Americans and especially most Protestants to think that these impersonal and apparently abstract ontological structures are relevant to, are in fact grounds of, deeply personal religious experience.

Time is, Tillich reminds us, a condition of our being and basic to it. If we *are*, we are in time. Positively, this means existence in the continuously new, and with that the ever-present possibility of a new, creative future grounded in our past. Here the experience of temporality is the source of new possibility, of promise, of confidence, and of joy in living. Negatively, however, being in time is a source of vast anxiety. The time we are in continually vanishes, and at an accelerated rate. We can neither stop its disappearance into the nonbeing of the past nor slow down its flow past us. We feel deeply and we share in that continual loss as when a weekend, a vacation, a time with our family, hurtles by into oblivion. As Plato said, the present we are in "never really is." When we ask anxiously *"When* are we?" we cannot answer, early this year, even this morning, even in the last minute. They are already gone. And yet the next moment is not yet here.

Time is thus as unreal as it is real; it slips away into nothingness. It is constituted only by the knife-edge of a vanishing present and then, finally, it has an end. We feel this with an undercoating of anxiety in our whole time. In class, Tillich went on: "You are too young to know this about your life, but let me remind you of the term paper. In October there is the infinity of time; in November we realize there is coming soon an end to our time; in December we are in ze panic!—and remember, this is true of your life, your being!" We sat there transfixed, recalling our own anxieties, and the many consequent efforts of humans to remain!

The next day, Tillich talked about space; we were all attention. Space is also a condition of our being; not to have space is not to be, and none of us have any space essentially or necessarily. All of us can be removed from any space; in the end we will be, and we know and feel this. Hence the gigantic importance of the *border* of our space—of our home, of our state, of our nation, space for our family, for our community, for our people, for us. Thus we are ever enlarging it, caring for it, *defending* it. One is at once struck by the immense relevance of this needless drive for space to every political and ethnic conflict. I recall now that when in 1948 I listened to Tillich in class in New York, I had seen again in my mind's eye the Jewish family in a grungy restaurant in Yokohama in 1940, as I was waiting for the boat to China. White-faced and nervous, looking continually over their shoulders, this family had been blown out eastward all the way to Japan from Nazi Germany, seeking space to be. And now Japan had just joined the Axis, and they had no space except the wide Pacific to the east! I saw and felt their deep anxiety then, but it was only later in Tillich's class that I understood what that angst was.

I also recalled people in our internment camp, fighting over inches of space in the dorm and secretly moving the beds two or three inches when everyone else was gone, or on other occasions, demanding their own small room—"Space so I can be," as one woman put it. We note that these are, if anything is, spiritual and religious issues with immense consequences for security and for personal and political life. Through them, we can see (1) how anxiety is a result of our finitude, (2) how anxiety leads almost inescapably toward sin, and (3) how important courage and groundedness are if we would be whole.

The anxiety of finitude, which we have begun to trace, and its relation to the divine ground, is not all there is to Tillich. There is also estrangement or the fall, where we lose touch with our infinite ground. And there is the promise and the gift of a new being, an essential humanity under the conditions of existence. These, too, are crucial issues for Tillich and central to his theological understanding. But they are far too much for this introduction, so we shall stop here.

8

tillich and the neoorthodox

As is well known, for all of his career, Paul Tillich had a running argument or controversy with the dialectical theologians, or the neoorthodox, as we second-generation students and followers called them. We regarded Tillich as one of them. They all rejected liberal progressivism, as did we of the war generation. But we knew there were important differences, not least because Reinhold Niebuhr was also our teacher and, while he and Tillich were fast friends, they did argue frequently about theology. I shall here try to enumerate and discuss the important points of theological disagreement—they did not at all disagree politically—between those "theologians of the Word" or "biblical theologians," as they called themselves, and Tillich. Karl Barth is, of course, the great and central figure among the former, but I would rather discuss those issues that dominated the theology of the first half of the century than Barth, great as he is. Tillich was my teacher and friend, as of course was Niebuhr. Hence in these remarks I shall state Tillich's position and defend it on these questions. It is not easy to be neutral on these central issues of theology if one wishes to stand somewhere oneself!

Tillich and the Biblical Theologians

I will begin with two stories about Tillich, both of them clearly expressing his point of view. The first is about Barth. Tillich liked to invite a few special students to his apartment to what he called a *privatissimum*, a quiet theological conversation accompanied by some splendid Moselle wine. One time we asked him about Barth. He put down his glass carefully and said with immense seriousness: "Venn you fight a dictator and he has swallowed up all of culture, zenn you wish to have Barth on your side to defend you; he gives you the ground on which to stand. But I was right about theology and correlation; all theology, even Barth's, reflects its culture, and so you had better think *theologically* about that. Also, I left Germany for the right reason: to protest the persecution of the Jews, and not to defend the Lutheran pulpit! Thirdly, he went home; I left home—*and* I left on an earlier train!" With that Tillich picked up his glass, smiled, and we resumed our conversation.

The second was an encounter with Reinhold Niebuhr. At a gathering in the common room with the students on the floor at their feet, Niebuhr was saying to Tillich that he should not mix ontology with biblical language or myth, lest he thereby unconsciously identify creation and fall, for which error the biblical theologians continually criticized Tillich. Both were in a very good humor. Finally, Tillich sighed, got up from his chair, pulled back his jacket sleeve, and looked at his watch. Niebuhr and we stared at him puzzled. Then Tillich said: "Venn vas it, Reinnie, zat good creation; and how long did it last until the fall? From twelve noon to dinner time? Or to 12:30, 12:15? Reinnie, if zere is no *time* there, zen you do not have simple myth. And if zere is not time between creation and fall, then you must identify them in some way or other. For both reasons, you need ontology, an understanding of space, time and world in which your no longer primitive myth makes some sense!" Reinnie knew well when he was beaten, so he scratched his bald head and laughed good-naturedly.

These two amusing and interesting stories go to the heart of Tillich's arguments about method with the biblical theologians. As Tillich here shows, all the neoorthodox, including

Barth, accepted the modern scientific understanding of nature and the modern historical understanding of history. They were not fundamentalists or creationists, for whom the stories of Genesis represented literal truth, and so for whom the universe is a scant six to ten thousand years old. Whether they wanted to or not, therefore, all of them joined their biblical categories—for example, creation and fall—to a modern understanding of the world, to a modern view of space, time, and nature. Thus, said Tillich, they had better understand that new worldview, which is now, whether they like it or not, a part of their theology, and understand it *theologically*. Ontology is a necessary part, if only a part, of a nonfundamentalist theology. Correlation of biblical symbols with our cultural and historical self-understanding is, therefore, quite unavoidable in all theology. And Tillich believed that, whatever they may say, all theologians, even Barth, were influenced by their historical and cultural context—in their understanding of creation by modern science, their understanding of history by the assumptions of modern historiography, of humans by modern psychology and sociology, and of the meaning of history by the terrible experience of World War I. Correlation, therefore, is inevitably going on in theology. Consequently, it is better to make its presence explicit, to defend and so be able to control it, than to ignore it and pretend it is not there. I agree with both of these arguments.

Ontological Issues

In his defense of ontology as an important aspect of theology, Tillich stressed two points that were vital to his theological self-understanding. The first is the relevance of religion to all the significant facets of our life. Tillich knew well the importance of the moral, of moral wrong and of guilt. The consciousness of sin and then of forgiveness—of "being accepted though we be unacceptable"—was the center of his Christian self-understanding, as were the anxiety of guilt and correspondingly the atonement. Nonetheless, there were for him other forms of deep anxiety than moral anxiety. There is the anxiety of temporality and of having to die, the anxiety of having no place or no space, the anxiety of unreality, of the loss of our being and of its ultimate loss in death. These too plague our life, and unless they are resolved, they drive us either to sin as hubris or to despair. These are for Tillich *religious* issues, matters of ultimate concern. The problems of death and of meaninglessness have dominated religious life as much as has guilt. To understand these forms of anxiety, we must understand at the deepest levels our bodily, psychic, and spiritual health. And in order to do that, we must understand the structure of our being, our essential nature and its distortion—and for Tillich, the central matter for ontology.

Ontology, as Tillich sees it, does not produce a general worldview irrelevant to issues of the spirit. It is the understanding of our own being as self in the world and self in community. And its theological purpose is not speculation but the comprehension in reflection of the problems, dilemmas, anxieties, and unwanted actions that dominate our lives and to which the message of *salus* (health), salvation, is the received answer. Hence Tillich defined our being ontologically as "finite freedom" and as "being bounded by non-being" in order accurately to comprehend the estrangement of our existence—its sin—and to comprehend the meaning of the rescue of our being in the new being that we receive in faith. As Socrates and then Augustine said, one does not need to understand sickness in order to feel sick; but precisely in order to heal our bodies, one must understand the structure of our body—and the same is true for spiritual health. Tillich used ontology not for speculative reasons but for religious and theological ones: to understand our being and its ailments in order to rescue it.

A second ontological issue central to the Christian message for Tillich is the status of God as the source, ground, and power of all being, including our being. God is, therefore, first of all Being-Itself and not *a* being among the beings. This was, of course, an ontological judgment that he thought crucial for sound theology. Interestingly, the reasons he gave for this ontological judgment were religious and theological, not philosophical, showing again for him the intimate relation and mutual dependence of ontology and theology. To be sure, he could have provided speculative, philosophical grounds for the assertion that God is Being-Itself, but the ones he cites were certainly religious.

There are two of these religious reasons for God's ultimacy. First, if God be a being over against us, then God is for Tillich the heteronomous Other, the Almighty and all-authoritative Ruler opposed to my being and to my autonomy, and as Nietzsche and many Buddhists have pointed out, a continual and inescapable threat to my freedom and dignity. Like the Romantics, Tillich could not stand such a monstrous deity, a feeling he shared deeply with many Buddhists. On the contrary, God is the ground and power of our being, as of all beings, the creative source and not the opponent of the autonomy of each. God is, therefore, the deep spring from which all the creativity of culture emerges. Our true ultimate concern, which is God, is thus not only the source of our religious faith, of our salvation, but as well the ground of the "secular" creativity of each person and of culture. For Tillich our relation to God is *theonomous*, not heteronomous. Hence, in God, religion and culture are one; religion as ultimate concern and the ultimate meaning in all that we do, is the substance of culture, and culture, the form of religion. I am not sure that either Nishitani or Tanebe understand this meaning of Being-Itself, namely, as the source of Suchness and not its opponent; to them, being is incurably finite and heteronomous, not ultimate and theonomous.

A further religious reason that God must be Being-Itself and not *a* being is that if God were a being among beings—and therefore finite—God would share with us the threat of nonbeing and all the dilemmas, anxieties, and unresolvable problems

of finitude. A purely temporal God would suffer, as we do, from
the anxiety of temporality, of having to die; a purely spatial
God would be able to lose God's space and vanish; a non-ultimate
God could in the end lose God's being, becoming unreal,
caused, and finally extinguished by nonbeing as are all finite
things. If God is to rescue us from unreality and extinction as
well as guilt—and this, Tillich reminds us, is the promise of the
gospel—God cannot be *a* being. Hence Tillich was wary of the
nonsymbolic use of the I–Thou, as for example, in the case of
Emil Brunner, although Tillich remained a fast friend of Martin Buber. For Tillich, Thou as the Other in personal encounter
is a valid *symbol* or analogy for God. But the more direct
speech is of God as Being-Itself, lest God become the sufferer
from finitude rather than its redeemer.

A Christomorphic Theologian

These are, I believe, impressive arguments, and they are religious and not philosophical. They have, however, understandably caused many to consider Tillich's theology, compared to
that of the biblical theologians, to be void of the personal or the
emphasis on God as a person and on ourselves as predomi-
nantly personal and moral beings. Although the reasons for
Tillich's insistence on God as Being-Itself are religious, nonetheless this seems to be a theological move that negates the personal in favor of the philosophical and thus, to many of the
neoorthodox, to seem to represent a non-Christian point of
view. However deeply Tillich understood the myth of the fall
and the wonder of revelation, still, if he negated the personal in
this way, how could his theology be considered either biblical
or Christian? I would like to contest this interpretation, perhaps the most fundamental argument the neoorthodox had
with Tillich. To grant unsymbolic and undialectical ultimacy to
the personal, God as an absolute Thou, seemed to Tillich on
religious grounds to be, as we have seen, counter to the most

important themes of biblical religion. But that granted, what role did Tillich give to the personal in his theology?

The personal for Tillich is encompassed in the word *spirit*, the category Tillich chose to refer to the uniqueness of the human as knower, as creator of culture, and as personal participant in community. Spirit begins with the centered self, where the capacity for knowledge, understanding, and judgment on the one hand appear, and where on the other the capacity for creative purposes and moral decisions becomes possible. Spirit is thus the seat of the human, the creative source of culture and of history, and the ground in ourselves of the moral and the religious. It is the place of the personal, of freedom, of uniqueness, and of intimacy. For Tillich, therefore, spirit unites in the human the power to be with the capacity for meanings and purposes; thus spirit represents the fullness of being. It is being now with inwardness, with intentions, purposes, and self-set goals, and hence with vast outward effect in reshaping both the natural and the social environments. We note that here, being is a category saturated with spirit; being is fulfilled in spirit. Thus it is not surprising to find Tillich saying that God as Being-Itself is also spirit: "Spirit is the most embracing, direct and unrestricted symbol for the divine Life" (Paul Tillich, *Systematic Theology*, vol. 1 [Chicago: University of Chicago Press, 1951–63] 249), hardly an impersonal conception either of being or of God.

Finally, the moral and the personal have a crucial role in the development of spirit as the seat of the human. For Tillich, the centered self integrates itself into a self in the moral act, in relation to a personal Other. In other words, it is in moral decision that the self becomes a person, aware of itself as responsible, aware of norms for its freedom, and above all, aware of its limits, of its finitude. It is, says Tillich, in an encounter with another self, an Other or a Thou over against us, not with the world, that we register inwardly our particularity and our

limit—our essential finitude. Hence there is a moral and personal constitution of the self; at its base, spirit is personal and
moral—and hence, of course, so is God as Spirit. God is Being,
Life, and Spirit for Tillich in an ascending order of importance.

The last point of basic disagreement between the biblical theologians, the theologians of the Word, is his seeming denial of the central role of the event of Christ. For Tillich, of
course, revelation of the ultimate and creative ground of all is
universal. And even an apprehension of the reconciling New
Being, bringing all of creation into a newly healing relation to
God, is universal. What role, then, for Tillich does the revelation in the Christ-event play? Clearly Tillich is not, as was
Barth, a christocentric theologian, that is, one for whom all
knowledge of God comes through the Christian revelation. But
he is also definitely not a natural theologian. And, further,
Tillich is clear that the symbol of the Christ provides the definitive understanding of the New Being, of human existence in
estrangement and in redemption alike, and, finally, the true
form for the church and for culture. In this sense, Tillich is a
christomorphic theologian: the revelation in Christ gives final
shape and definition to all knowledge of God and all relation-
ship to God—and that covers everything.

For Tillich, everything is a vehicle or symbol of the
ground and power of all being, God; hence revelation is universal. But the true symbol, that creaturely being which reflects a
valid and creative relation to God is one that, while remaining
in constant unity with its divine ground, nonetheless continually points beyond itself and criticizes and even negates itself.
Thus it does not glorify itself but only the transcendent divine
through which it lives. Clearly this is a picture or paradigm
derived from the picture of Jesus as the Christ in the New Testament. That picture, therefore, defines not only the true
Christian life but also the church. The true form of the church,
says Tillich, is one that unites a Catholic substance—intrinsic
unity with the divine in sacramental presence—with the

Protestant principle, the continual self-criticism of the ecclesia and the continual pointing beyond itself to the mystery of God. Furthermore, this is also for Tillich the true analogical paradigm for culture, namely, one that nurtures and encourages its ultimate concerns—for art, economic and political justice, and knowledge: its forms of culture. Yet it is also a culture critical of the hubris that claims finality for its own cultural achievements. This is, needless to say, a *theonomous* culture, one inspired by the sacred presence of the divine in its ultimate concerns, and yet one guarding carefully the genuine autonomy of each of its aspects. If, as Tillich insisted, religion is the substance of culture, then a valid cultural life reflects the pattern of this christomorphic symbol. No theologian, it seems to me, has interpreted church and culture in a more biblical fashion than this, not only as at base religious but as ideally christomorphic.

9

american theology
since niebuhr and tillich

Our subject here is American theology since Reinhold Niebuhr and Paul Tillich or, roughly speaking, American theology in the last half century. I must confess that after these two giants there occurs a rather sharp drop in quality. I should know; I am part of the generation that followed! There are, of course, a number of distinguished names: Gordon Kaufman, Sallie McFague, John Cobb, Schubert Ogden, and, of course, David Tracy. Still, I think it is more interesting and illuminating to discuss new issues in American theology than persons, issues that have arisen only after these two seminal figures, Niebuhr and Tillich, left the scene in the early 1960s. I shall discuss three issues: pluralism of religion, ecology and nature, and finally the fundamentalist revival. As I said, each of these issues entered public and theological consciousness since their time—though at the end of his life in the early 1960s, Tillich felt the force of the problem of pluralism, especially in relation to Buddhism.

First, however, let me say a brief word about what seems to be the situation since the middle of the twentieth century. The radical relativity of culture—of science, philosophy, and religion alike—was taken for granted by all the neoorthodox or dialectical theologians; their experience of two world wars had taught them this, and (to me) they each built their theologies in part on the firm ground of historical relativism. However, they all shared a confidence in the objectivity of revelation, even if the human faith, the theology, and the religion that responded to it remained relative. This sense of the objectivity of revelation has, it seems to me, dissipated, certainly for many reasons. Our half century continued in part—even if unremarked—the strange "God is dead" phenomenon that flashed across the sky in 1960–64. The sense of relativism has vastly increased since, expressed if not caused by postmodernism, which added itself to this growth of skepticism. As a result, theological statements are more hazardous and theological construction more difficult. The confident expression of the "biblical viewpoint" that characterized the theologians of the Word or of a possible system of universal understanding that certainly characterized Whitehead and in part Tillich seems centuries and not decades ago. It is well to remember this general pattern as we discuss our three issues.

Religious Pluralism

One of the stated war aims of the Japanese military expansion that nearly engulfed Asia in 1941–42 was the expulsion from Asia of the European empires that then ruled almost everything in the Orient; as was repeatedly said: "Asia for the Asiatics." This aim, interestingly, was thoroughly achieved. Each one of the empires—France, the Netherlands, and especially Britain, disintegrated shortly after the war. In their places have appeared throughout Asia autonomous cultures—politically, culturally, and especially religiously. The tremendous power of the West, economically, politically, and in popular culture, remains, but it no longer represents direct political and economic rule as it once did. Above all, the cultural and religious dominance of the West—hitched to the false view on both sides of the superiority of the modern West—has receded. As one result, the predominance and so-called superiority of Christianity have also receded since they were based, more than the theologians realized, on the military, economic, and political power of the West! This has left room for the revitalization, in intellectual, moral, and spiritual power of each of the religions of Asia. The consequence has been a quite new balance of power, so to speak, among the religions. Effective missionary work now flows the other way, from East to West; dialogue between religions has become common; and some sort of "rough parity" is now more or less taken for granted among Christian leaders.

Many interesting, unexpected, and very positive results— besides genuine verbal and intellectual dialogue—have come from this new world of relations. In the West, in the nineteenth and twentieth centuries, the moral conscience and behavior of the ordinary citizen—not the monk—was at the center of religious consciousness. As a consequence, the antislavery movement, the social gospel, and liberationist theology appeared and dominated liberal theology and neoorthodoxy alike—and immediately were passed on to the religions of Asia. However, the older modes of personal piety, while remaining among the liberals, vanished among our neoorthodox generation. Patterns of personal piety became almost extinct except among conservatives. This helps perhaps to explain the new and astounding interest in mysticism in the West. Mysticism had been scorned by the liberals as otherworldly, politically and socially unconcerned, a kind of selfish cop-out, and by the neoorthodox as "unhistorical." In the present, however, the mystical is, I believe, the dominant form of religious piety in the West, among Christians, among new converts to Zen or Vedanta, and among secular but inwardly concerned people unconnected with any tradition. I have noted that most people now become interested in religion not through the arguments of Buddhist philosophers or Christian theologians but through doing Zazen or yoga. This is a vast change.

Dialogue between religions is exciting and challenging, and if each regards it as a most creative and enlightening

conversation rather than an excuse for apologetics, it is not difficult. However, it does raise important, even unsettling, theological problems, of which all of us who have done dialogue these
last decades are uncomfortably aware! The problem I refer to is
simple enough: Christian faith, and all of its theological expressions—however historically relative they may be—are grounded
in the absoluteness and the uniqueness of the event of revelation
to which our faith is a response. Likewise in Buddhism, while all
symbols and reflection are relative, nonetheless everything depends on the absoluteness and uniqueness of the higher consciousness. If, in either case, another religious position enters the
scene, as it does in dialogue, then apparently this absolute
ground is compromised. The Torah, the Koranic revelation, or
the Christ-event is no longer the only center of valid religion, the
one absolute revelation of God, but one way, and only one among
many, into the mystery of the divine. And the Buddhist higher
consciousness takes its place among other forms of consciousness
as helpful, illuminating, but not ultimate. I have not met any
Christians or Buddhists happy with this consequence!

Many who have clearly seen this dilemma—for example, John Hick or Wilfred Smith—have suggested that faith and
theology must be founded not on one religious tradition but on
a universal religious basis. But then this new ground itself turns
out to be particular—for example, a particular form of Western
(or Eastern) moral theism, which is less universal than, say,
Buddhism. There is no escape for us through thought or action
from particularity: we are incurably finite, and each of our perspectives remains partial. And perhaps this point can be a clue
for us: "the true symbol," said Tillich, is true and universal only
if it, on the one hand, stays in continual contact with its divine
ground, but on the other hand only if it also continually criticizes, negates, and judges itself and so points beyond itself to the
mystery of the divine. This theme, resonant in Christianity and
Buddhism alike, well expresses the religious and intellectual
basis of dialogue: continual fidelity to one's own standpoint,

criticism of it, pointing beyond it, and recognizing the validity and the relevance of another stance. The new theological question, unresolved as yet, is whether the center of a particular religious tradition can *also* relativize itself and point beyond itself. There is nowhere a better place than Japan, where significant Buddhist and Christian forces meet and converse, for this problem to be resolved.

Ecology and Nature

Our second issue is the question of nature. This, too, is a new question. Theology in the first half of the last century concentrated on history and its meaning, and theologians more or less ignored nature, as did most of Western culture. This is not surprising. Their time faced an unsurpassed chaos in history: two great wars inspired by aggressive and oppressive regimes, a chaos that challenged totally the belief in historical progress that had dominated nineteenth- and early-twentieth-century culture. Our present, since roughly 1960, faces a different, if equally severe, crisis; this time the crisis of an endangered nature. Nature is now threatened by the technical dominance over nature of modern society, a society driven by the ruthless expansion of our industrial and commercial civilization, by what Buddhists call *desire* and Christians call *concupiscence.* Hence, since about 1970, every theologian has become concerned with the problem of ecology and the question of a theology of nature, namely, how our religious faith views, understands, and values nature. We should note, however, that while now theology is occupied with the status and preservation of nature, the source of the problem of nature lies in history, namely, in the use and misuse that a creative and intelligent, and thus dangerous, humankind makes of nature. Advanced technology now makes it possible for greedy humans to destroy nature—and thus themselves. A history characterized by sin has, therefore, finally come to endanger nature. Thus, in a quite new context, we have returned to the problem that beset the theologians of a century ago, the problem of sin.

The preservation of nature is a most complex matter. It is a scientific and technological issue initially, but it is also an industrial and commercial question and thus a vastly explosive economic and political issue where great economic powers confront environmental forces. Finally, therefore, it is a moral and religious question. Needless to say, the inherited conflict between an objectivist science and a traditional and, so, mythological understanding of religion—both of them difficult for ecology—has not helped. Fortunately there has developed meanwhile a new philosophy of science that sees science as a human mode of interpreting nature, which while amazingly accurate and helpful, is still perspectival and composed of images and models. Thus science is now, as seldom before, amenable to discussion with morals, philosophy, and religion. Much of the rest of the theology of our period has been devoted to this discussion.

A second influence on a theology of nature has been the increasing importance of evolutionary thought on theological construction. Most of the great neoorthodox thinkers accepted scientific thought: on the age of the universe, on the long cosmic history of constant changes, and on the evolutionary origin and development of human beings. They were neither fundamentalists nor creationists. Nonetheless, none of them developed their theologies with an eye to these scientific matters but only, as noted, to the actions of humans in history in relation to one another and to God. In our present, in contrast, there is hardly a constructive theology that does not develop its conception of God and its understanding of human beings very much under the influence of cosmology, and especially, the genetic and evolutionary understanding of human beings. One could say—I am here speaking for myself—that most theology has embraced the new symbolic and relativistic self-understanding of science, especially its use of models, and the newly reinforced understanding of nature as continually undergoing radical change, to form a new sort of theological understanding, quite different from the "biblical theologies," even that of Tillich, of the first half of the last century.

We note that while the new emphasis on radical change or temporality is a point long made by process thought, the present even greater emphasis on symbolism, models, and relativity in metaphysics and theology alike is not compatible with classical process thinking. Needless to say, out of this new union of science, philosophy of science, and theology have come a number of interesting and persuasive "natural theologies": Paul Davies, Arthur Peacocke, John Polkinghorne, Robert Russell, Philip Hefner, and even the present writer, to name a few.

The problem of nature, we have said, combines scientific, technological, economic, and political issues—but it is also at base a moral and a religious question. If we would save nature and so ourselves, we must cease to exploit nature for our own purposes. And that in turn means we must begin to respect nature's integrity and value for herself and not merely for us. We must see nature as an end in itself and not just as a means to our ends or wants. These are moral questions calling for our strongest moral courage. Thus are they also religious questions, questions of our deepest attitudes toward ourselves and nature, matters of ultimate concern. As the history of the human exploitation and misuse of other humans shows, we have only begun to treat other humans as ends when, on the level of our deepest commitments, we regard them differently. For example, humans have in modern times been more moral to one another only when they saw others as of infinite value, as made in the divine image.

Many of us, therefore, have begun to speak of nature not only as the creation of God but also as made in the divine image, that is: as a mirror, a sign, or a symbol of God as are we. Although this is not a part of the historical tradition, this has good biblical precedent, especially directly in the psalms and in Job. In a more general sense, however, it is very clear that for our entire tradition, nature has been a most significant mirror, sign, or symbol of the divine, of God as we understand God. Where else could our sense of infinity and of ultimate mystery, of the ultimate power we associate with God, have arisen except through our experience of the infinity, ultimacy, and power of nature around us and in us? And where else could our sense of a ruling Order, an ultimate and divine Logos at the heart of all there is, have arisen except from the experience of the continual and universal order of nature, in its changes and its repetitions alike? And since God is for us not only ultimate Power and Order but also Life, the vibrant spirit-giving power in all living things, certainly this trait as the Living God has come from our life in nature. To be sure, the biblical and Christian God is primarily the Lord of history, of communities, and of personal life. Nonetheless, these most fundamental categories of Power, Order, and Life, the ground and basis of our conception of God, are mirrored in nature before they are or can be seen in the ups and downs of history. Nature is an image of God. Hence, as much as we, nature deserves our respect and care as an end in itself and not just a means. I think nowhere on earth is this more deeply felt and believed than in Japan, and in no religion is it more clearly experienced and expressed than in Shinto.

The Fundamentalist Revival

I shall be brief with our last issue, the rise of fundamentalism, though it is too important to our present religious situation to omit. Again, fundamentalism was not a problem in the first half of the twentieth century. Secular ideologies—fascism, communism, nationalism, and capitalism, not religious fanaticism—disturbed theologians of this era. Also they—and we—agreed with Rudolf Bultmann that a technological civilization (for example, as he said, "listening by radio to the weather forecast") would gradually undercut throughout the culture any religious-mythological view of natural reality, such as the belief that rain is the result of a divine command. In this, we were quite obviously completely wrong. It is in the advanced technological cultures of our present era that religious fundamentalism has almost everywhere grown. For example, a creationist understanding of nature as created only ten thousand years ago thrives in an American culture based throughout on scientific technology! Furthermore, previous fundamentalists were not *theocratic*, that is, intent on capturing and ruling civic society according to their own religious laws and doctrines. Now, in almost all cultures where a religious tradition is predominant—in some Islamic cultures, in Israel, possibly in India—and as the long-term aim of the Christian Coalition in America, a strong and threatening theocratic movement flourishes.

How are we to understand this, we who support religion but have learned now also to fear it? All of the neoorthodox also feared the dogmatism, intolerance, and utter cruelty of which the fanatical religion of the past was capable, but none of them felt this to be an active threat in advanced areas of present modern culture. We do. Clearly the development of modern culture has had as a major consequence the gradual dissolving of religious certainties and their accompanying absolute moral principles. This dissolving process initially occurred when modern culture penetrated into new lands with ancient religious and moral structures. Surprisingly, however, it has also happened where the scientific and technological culture originated. In such cultures, too, older religious and moral certainties have been threatened, if not pushed completely aside. Such a process clearly has for us its creative side; older prejudices, forms of racial and gender domination and injustice, and dogmatic intolerance have receded. But we should be aware—as Tillich reminds us—of the dangers that accompany the growth of autonomy. The vanishing of sacred certainties leaves a vast void, and then, if that dissolving is intense enough, the sacred returns, this time with crushing authority and intolerance. A repressive religious regime—whether in the

name of Islam, Judaism, true Hinduism, or Christian fundamentalism and family values—can appear. Surprisingly but
evidently many for whom the beliefless and normless culture of
modernity is void of meaning and security welcome that return
of the sacred, support it, and seek to banish the autonomy they
now fear. As our current history shows, the passage to a more
liberal, more tolerant, and more moral world is fraught with
danger, the danger of the angry return of the defenders of the
old order! I suspect that Japan has experienced some form of
this same problem; it has been, I can assure you, a surprise to
optimistic America to find itself plagued by it.

Two things can be said. First, the moral authority of customs, of law, and of social practices must be grounded in a
religious sense of ultimacy. Secular autonomy does unravel
unless the autonomous realms of art, literature, science, philosophy, and the social practices of economic and political life
have a *theonomous* depth, a ground in religious understanding
and commitment. The function of religion is absolutely vital in
and for the world, but not as the judge, legislator, and ruler of
social existence, as the theocrats believe. Profound religion
supports cultural autonomy; it does not rule it. In the world,
the ultimate criteria for religion are freedom and justice, not
compliance to authority. Further, religion must be critical of itself as well as of society, lest it become more demonic than the
secularism it opposes.

Finally, in our country at least, it is probably our vast
diversity, the autonomy and freedom of many different traditions and religious voices, that will—if anything will—save
us. It will be not our virtue or our wisdom but the plurality of
attitudes and opinions that will make theocracy impossible, if
we are spared theocracy. This may be something the Christian
community in Japan will wish to remember: to ally themselves with, and not oppose, the many other minority voices
that animate this great culture!

Part 3
Hopeful Illuminations

10

plurality and its theological implications

Our subject in this chapter is the impingement of the plurality of religions on theology or, more accurately stated, the effect of the present sense or understanding of plurality on theology. The churches have always known that religions are plural, that there are other religions than our own. This consciousness of plurality raised few theological problems since the church was convinced on a number of grounds that Christianity was the only truly valid religion, the only effective "way." That we now speak of theological implications of plurality, and clearly intend *serious* implications, thus bespeaks a new sense or understanding of plurality, a new assessment of its meaning. This new understanding, therefore, includes and adds the concept of "parity," or of "rough parity," to that of plurality. We recognize, often against our will, that in some sense the sole efficacy or even the superiority of Christianity is a judgment we can no longer make, or can make only with great discomfort. I assume we are all agreed on this; otherwise, a serious discussion of diversity and its theological meaning would not be undertaken, nor would serious and authentic dialogue between religions be possible.

From Superiority to Parity

When we ask what the causes are of this new understanding of plurality as rough parity, we find both theological and cultural causes. The latter, I think, are definitive. Let us begin with the theological. What is there in recent developments of Christian theology that has helped to encourage this recognition of the co-validity and the co-efficacy of other religions? These same developments have fostered the new views of each other by the various churches, that is, the ecumenical movement; new ways of relating to Jews; new conceptions of relations between diverse races and between the sexes, and new interpretations of Christian obligations toward the world. In short, strong diversity on many fronts has gradually over the past century and half come to be viewed differently by Christian groups than previously. Now that the relations to other religions have moved center stage, these theological developments have been effective there also.

The most important is the shift in balance between what were called the requirements of faith and those of love, or better put, a new assessment of how God views these requirements. Previously, "defending the faith" and its purity (defending its doctrinal purity), and so defending that purity against other religious viewpoints, was regarded as an unquestioned Christian demand, one that clearly outranked the obligation to love the other (see Calvin in relation to Servetus). In the modern period, largely with the help of the Enlightenment, this dominance of faith over love shifted. Love became the major obligation, and the person who killed in defense of the purity of faith was regarded not so much as a Christian hero but as morally dubious, as a misguided fanatic. Correspondingly, and through many of the same cultural forces, the doctrines of faith—creeds, confessions, and even the words of the Scripture itself—began to be seen as human, as therefore historical and relative expressions of a truth that transcended any single expression. Their defense is thus no longer the defense of God, and again the defense becomes morally dubious. These two shifts were largely accomplished by Protestant liberalism. It is, therefore, no surprise that the first ecumenical rapprochement began under the aegis of that theological period as did the first large-scale recognition of the truth and validity of other religions. It is also no surprise that those churches that have not at all participated in the Enlightenment and in the liberal theology that grew out of it have no interest in—in fact, have distrust of—the ecumenical movement in all its phases. And they defend with every means available the absolute truth of their own doctrines and the sole efficacy of their modes of salvation.

One other theological factor is relevant, since the neoorthodox movement continued, with only a few qualifications, the ecumenical spirit established by liberalism. Why? First, despite their emphasis on the finality and uniqueness of Christian revelation, the neoorthodox nevertheless accepted the relativity of doctrine, confessions, and laws—the realm of "religion" in Barth's sense—and also they seconded the priority of love over the demands of doctrinal faith. Even more important, I suggest, was the fact that they combined that relative assessment of the externals of religion, including doctrinal and legal exactness, with a vast emphasis on the inwardness of religion and on justification by faith. It was central to their interpretation of Christianity that salvation came through neither perfection of life nor perfection of faith, for they recognized their own fallibility in both. All that we have or can give, then, is relative. Whatever the partiality or the waywardness of our religious life, all must be and has been justified by an alien grace; neither our works nor our faith will here suffice.

To those who said this—that the agape of God covers all the relativity, especially the religious relativity, of their existence, and that the inward commitment and love in their life are all that is significant—it was inconceivable that suddenly this should stop, and stop, so to speak, at the boundary of the Christian church. Could the divine agape choose us because of the external "religion" in which we live and not reach out to others because of the external religion in which they grew up and which they now affirm? Is not this same all-encompassing love that justifies *my* paltry relative faith capable of justifying another different but also relative faith provided, as Søren Kierkegaard said, that they are inwardly serious? Can the divine love base itself on religious any more than on social or moral externals? In this case, am I not justified by my work of Christian belief, poor as it is? Thus agape so interpreted suddenly overflowed the bounds of one tradition and expanded to include others beyond the now relative bounds of the church: Jews, authentic secular saints, and committed members of other traditions. The relativity of religion and its doctrines, plus the reemphasis on the width of the divine love, plus the inwardness of faith and love, have been the theological sources of this new assessment of plurality.

Important as these theological developments were, it has been the cultural changes that the twentieth century witnessed that have represented the major causes of the development of parity. The theological changes just mentioned were enough to force the *inclusion* of other religions into the area of truth and of grace, if I may so put it. Liberals and most neoorthodox alike admitted this: God revealed himself elsewhere, and his grace is present there (as is well known, Barth's position is strangely ambiguous on this). However, liberals and most neoorthodox alike—from Schleiermacher and Ritschl through the dialectical theologians Bultmann, Brunner, the Niebuhrs, and Tillich— also retained a sense of what Schleiermacher called "the absoluteness of Christianity," or what they would rather term the superiority, finality, and absolute uniqueness of the revelation in Christ. Few recognized the kind of parity with which we began, except of course vis-à-vis (for example, for Tillich and the Niebuhrs) the Jews. My suggestion is, therefore, that cultural changes since their period (the 1920s, 1930s, and 1940s) have effected the further move toward parity, from Christianity as the definitive revelation among other revelations to some sort of plurality of revelations—a monstrous shift indeed.

My point is that historically Western culture has recently undergone precisely this same shift: from a position of clear superiority to one of rough parity, and that this shift in cultural consciousness has in turn had a vast effect on our theological consciousness, namely, the parallel shift toward parity. The West had been dominant in almost every sphere, at almost every level, for four centuries: militarily, scientifically, industrially, politically, sociologically, morally, and religiously—or at least of that dominance, the West had no doubt. Together—as *Passage to India* shows—this total domination up and down the line, a domination over each of these spheres, created an unbelievable assumption of superiority—not the first such sense in world history but surely one as absolutely certain as any preceding one! This lasted through the neoorthodox period: World War II. Such a grandiose superiority carried everything along with it: morals, democracy, religion, customs—all. And again, as *Passage to India* shows, its devastating character is shown by the fact that it was *assented to* by many of those who were demeaned by it—by Indians, Japanese, and Chinese alike. To them there was hardly any point at which they could claim even parity, much less superiority—hence their vast repressed anger, evident in the depth of their successive reactions against the West.

After 1945, this superiority began to collapse, and to collapse on all of these levels: military, political, moral, and religious. Colonies vanished, Europe disappeared as a major power, other non-Western power centers appeared representing other ways of life and other religions. The West no longer ruled the world; Western ways were no longer unassailable; Western religion became one among the other world religions and (not insignificantly) the one now most morally culpable, the chief imperialistic, nonspiritual, and in fact barely moral faith! Correspondingly, Western culture became radically open to non-Western religions. Missionary influence flowed in the opposite direction, and the spiritual power of other faiths began to assert itself on Christian turf. Here were vast changes from even forty years earlier: Christianity now stood not as the accuser but as the morally accused by other religions. At home it found itself passive, almost dried up and lifeless in relation to vibrant and effective other religions around it, and Christian families had to deal with the conversion of their members into other traditions.

This dramatic new situation has forced—and this is the right word I think—a new understanding of the interrelations of religions, a new balance of spiritual power on all, a sense of ascending equality if not superiority on the part of other religions, and a sense of descending status, lucky if it achieves equality, on the part of on many Christians. It is this that has pushed us all into parity, a position quite new to the churches, even the liberal churches. Thus, as always, religious changes and cultural changes appear and recede together, and neither can be understood out of relation to the other. All this is of no little significance also to the secular academy that regards our discovery of religious parity among the world's religions as a kind of childlike awakening from naïveté and self-centeredness. And yet the same academy has not even conceived the shock that is to come to it when the cultural parity of the West, among the world's other cultures, comes to the forefront of consciousness. The plurality of cultures viewed as parity rather than as an ascending series up to our scientific and liberal culture is just around the corner; it has already been and still is effective in theological reflection in the area of religion.

Particularity and Universality

Plurality as parity, we said, has devastating theological effects—or at least I believe it should have. To be sure, this new situation is fascinating, in Rudolf Otto's sense at once alluring and threatening. To recognize, as one does or must in dialogue the presence of truth and of grace, the validity of symbol and efficacy of practice, in another faith is radically to relativize not only one's own religious faith but the referent of that faith, the

revelation on which it is dependent. Thus to be in dialogue is
also to be driven on a new theological quest, namely, the effort
to interpret one's symbols so as to neither exclude nor offend
this other. That is to say, in dialogue some mode of new theological self-understanding is necessary, an understanding that
includes and supplements what the other offers instead of rejecting it as false or incorporating it as merely one vista in the
panorama shaped by one's own viewpoint. The liberal effort to
seem to include and so to incorporate—for the two go together—thus begins to seem to be the imperial effort to take
over, absorb, and dominate (not unlike a colonial domination
in order to "raise" the other). Note that this quest—the present central one of theology—is more radical than that of
"modernizing," "demythologizing," or even "re-presenting" or
"revising." The latter relativized only past expressions; far
more radical, painful, and yet exciting is to relativize the
symbols themselves. And that is the newness of our situation.

Let us, then, begin to think about these theological effects, for that is about all we can as yet do. The first important
point to make is that the problematic involves *all* theological
doctrines, not just some of them; it is not that only the symbols
of revelation and Christology are at issue so that a more liberal
understanding of revelation and of Christ, perhaps the elimination of these altogether, will resolve it. Several such efforts
have appeared—for example, that of John Hick. For then one
is left with God the creator, moral ruler, and presumably redeemer as well. Unfortunately, such a classical theism is as
particular as is any orthodox theology; it is Semitic and Western in form, strikingly different from Hindu, Buddhist, or
Confucian conceptions. Each system of religious symbols
forms a coherent, interrelated whole; and each gestalt of symbols is particular, at variance with other gestalten. Thus each
doctrine or symbol within any given system differs signifi-
cantly from analogous symbols in other systems. As a result,
no one doctrine in any such system of symbols (again, for

example, God or human being) can be abstracted out and established as universal in all religions, a point of unity with other religious traditions. God is as similar—*and* as different—from the ultimate principals of Hinduism and Buddhism as are the Christ and Krishna or the Christ and a bodhisattva.

Nor is there a philosophical way to transcend these particularities and achieve a universal standpoint, a standpoint above and neutral to the fundamental differences between religions. It is possible to translate the religious symbols of a given tradition into fundamental metaphysical terms, though—as the efforts of Hegel and Whitehead show—much there is lost as well as gained. Such philosophical systems, however, reveal themselves in the end to be as particular as were the theologies they absorbed and transcended. The particularity in this case is, of course, that of a *culture*—in this case, Western culture— rather than that of a certain religious tradition. Thus, to the philosopher, and to the academy where he or she works, there appears the illusion of a new universality, the universality of the culture as a whole as opposed to the partiality of the church within the culture. But looked at on the scale relevant here, we find that modern Western philosophy is as particular, as located in space and time, as are the Christian and the Buddhist traditions—and that philosophy is as alien from the corresponding philosophies of India and China as the relevant sets of religious symbols are from one another. Recent decades have shown us clearly that no religious tradition is universal, and as a consequence, that its claims to be so distort rather than express its message. The coming decades, I am sure, will reveal that Western culture, which certainly thought it was universal, is also not so—and that its claims, and the claims of its modes of philosophy, to universality and finality will soon seem as ludicrous as were the same claims of religion.

If dispensing with or toning down certain doctrines (revelation and Christology) does not work, and if translation into metaphysical categories does not work, what does? The other familiar—and to me more fruitful—move is to try to find a religious or theological mode of universality: an interpretation of the religious symbols themselves that is inclusive of other traditions. I shall mention two. The first effort, pioneered by Schleiermacher and continued by Tillich and most of the more liberal neoorthodox, is to propose on the one hand a wide understanding of general revelation through which the truth and the grace evident in other religions (and cultures) can be theologically explicated, and on the other some form of universal salvation through which the efficacy of these other religious ways can be affirmed. Thus are other religions included as valid and effective within a Christian theology of revelation and incarnation. In all of these, however, Christian revelation remains "final and definitive," to use Tillich's words—it is the Christian God of justice and love who saves all who are saved. While Christian revelation is thus no longer exclusive, it does still claim to represent the final and universal criterion for all faiths; instead, it provides the principle through which they are more validly interpreted than when they are interpreted on their own terms. This mode is called "inclusion."

This is, I believe, formally and precisely the method used by Hinduism and Buddhism. Recognizing other religions as valid ways to the truth, they nevertheless use their own version of mystical pantheism to define how far each of the others progresses on the true way, how far they each climb up, so to speak, the *real* mountain. And they regard the higher consciousness through which their understanding appears, and the symbols appropriate to that consciousness, as the only way finally that reality can be known and understood. In both the Christian and the mystical versions, however, these efforts—and I must admit to using them myself—*now* seem to remain parochial, inadequate to the new situation. For each incorporates others into its own world, interprets and defines them from an alien perspective, as when Christianity or Judaism are seen by mystical religions as "really" mystical. Thus, in effect, such interpretation deconstructs them, transforming them into something they are not. One can hardly carry on a dialogue on this basis—for each, in seeing the other through his own eyes, can never hear what the other has to say.

The second form of this effort is to me the more interesting, although I find its theological implications very alien indeed. I refer to the attempt to interpret all religions as particular expressions of a perennial religious-philosophical center, or as Fritjhof Schuon terms them, exoteric manifestations of an esoteric heart. There is, he says, a mystical core of each religion, a core that can be grasped by intellect and articulated in a philosophy of absolutism. This universal core is participated in and borne by an elite in each religion. The exoteric or outer clothing of each of the religions—its particular gestalt of symbols, its moral laws, sacraments, and liturgical customs—is *revealed*, since the divine understands that not all men and women are elite, and that different cultures need different religious homes, so to speak. Thus each particular religion is *true* and yet *relative*, a true revelation for that community, relative to other true revelations to other communities, and relative to the Absolute, which each only partially and so somewhat distortedly manifests. Clearly the ultimacy and finality are here drained from the Christian revelation, the Jewish law, the Koran, the Four Noble Truths, and so on, and a fortiori theology is reduced to an in-house exercise. Only the mystical core within each tradition and its philosophical expression in absolutism remain of universal relevance. As the first alternative, centered in general as distinct from special revelation, raised a particular tradition above all the others, so now this second resolution raises an *aspect* of religion (mysticism) and its philosophical equivalent to supreme status over other aspects of the religious. Thus other religions, centered in those aspects—for example, commitment and obedience to the divine will, creative political action for justice, sacramental and liturgical participation in a sacramental community, and so on—are reduced to the relativity of the mere exoteric. As in the first form, the Christian incorporates the Buddhist and the Hindu into her perspective, so here the mystical incorporates the non-mystical into an alien framework. In neither case is universality achieved, and in neither case is dialogue possible.

Interestingly, in each of these recent efforts at genuine ecumenicity, some element of absolutism clearly remains. In the first, Christian revelation, now inclusive of all others, retains its "final" status; in the second, the mystical alone is non-relative. If, then, both of these resolutions are found wanting and discarded, as I feel they must be, then clearly in so doing the last hold against relativity appears to be relinquished. If no revelation is held to be finally valid, how is any truth to be known unless one retreats to science, philosophy, or common sense and so embraces the alternative absolutism of Western culture? If no one aspect of religion is absolute but all aspects are relative, what now are the bases for confidence in religion itself? There seems to be here nowhere solid to stand, either in a given tradition and its symbols or in religious experience and its various aspects. And note, this is real relativism: here, if they are relativized—God, Christ, grace, and salvation; higher consciousness, dharma, nirvana, and *mukti*—they all begin to recede in authority, take on the aspect of mere projections relative to the cultural and individual subjectivity of the projectors, and so in the end vanish like bloodless ghosts. We have no grounds for speaking of salvation at all, which represents a situation of relativity far beyond asking about the salvation of *all*. A slide toward radical relativity has appeared, and any theological basis we might suggest for stopping that slide also begins itself to slide. The rough parity of religions, by removing the absolute starting point of each, seems to drain each of whatever it has to say and give to us and so to leave us empty— void of moves to some other more solid ground. Ecumenical tolerance represents an impressive moral and religious gain, a step toward love and understanding. But it has its own deep risks, one of which is this specter of relativity, this loss of any place to stand, this elimination of the very heart of the religious as ultimate concern.

The Complexity and Ambiguity of Plurality

As we have seen, plurality drives in the direction of ecumenical tolerance. Plurality, however, has another face, a face fully as terrifying as the relativity just described, for among the plurality of religions that surround us are forms of the religions that are intolerable, and intolerable because they are demonic. Toleration is here checked by the intolerable, and plurality means both.

We have always seen this aspect of diversity out of the corner of the eye. We know there were religious cannibals, religious sacrifices of human victims, religious wars of aggression, religious murders, religious castes—and so on. Most of these have in our consciousness been pushed aside through the need, and it is a real need, to be tolerant and to free religion from its baleful fault of intolerance, of fanaticism, and of infinite cruelty. But this, too, was dialectical—and twentieth-century experience has also shown this point aplenty. For in the last century, intolerable forms of religion and the religious have appeared: in a virulently nationalistic Shinto, in Nazism, in aspects of Stalinism and Maoism, in Khomeini—and in each of these situations an absolute religion has sanctioned an oppressive class, race, or national power. These forms represent the "shadow side" of religion, and they are infinitely destructive. When faced with one of them, we must resist, and we must liberate ourselves and others from them.

This danger implicit in plurality, namely, that demonic possibilities lie within even the religions of our land, has appeared before us in the recent rise to considerable political power of the Religious Right. To be sure, like the poor they scorn, the Religious Right have always been with us. But in recent times, they have moved from the fringes of our culture close to the centers of political power, and—as usually happens—their political demands have consequently vastly increased. Mind you, I do not think them to be an immediate danger. The countering forces of pluralism in religion and in lifestyle are too great, the mainline churches and the academies too strong, and the Constitution is for the time unchanged. Still, if the level of anxiety within our common life rises, surprising things can happen, as they have happened to other cultures repeatedly in the last century: Japan, Germany, Italy, Russia, China, Iran, to name a few. Despite our confidence in ourselves, we are by no means immune to this disease, and when the fever of anxiety gets high enough, even constitutional guards, not to mention diversity of custom and of ecclesiastical centers, may not be sufficient.

I bring up the Religious Right, however, to illustrate the complexity and ambiguity of plurality, and to point to the dialectical opposition, even the paradoxes and contradictions, that is latent within diversity. For like the cases of Hitler and Khomeini, the Religious Right represents something we cannot tolerate. I do not mean that we cannot tolerate their fundamentalist theology; we can and have to. I refer rather to their stated goal of theocracy, of establishing a "Christian America": a national community in which Christianity is the preferred religion; in which "Christians" are placed in crucial political roles; in which a certain sort of religious observance permeates the public sphere like in schools and in public places; in which fundamentalist doctrine dominates the teaching of science, social science, and history, as they intend; and in which the supremacy of the nation is identified totally with the will and the aims of God. As Jerry Falwell has said: "It is high time that Christians take back the power to run their own country," and "The constitution in the hands of Christians is a holy document: in the hands of non-Christians it can be used by the devil to defeat us." Here religion takes over and uses the public sphere; here religion, and the absolutist politics it spawns, manifests an intolerable face, as the secular religion of Nazism did. Against such religion—traditional or secular—resistance is necessary.

Now the point is that in order to resist—and we must, paradoxically on ecumenical grounds, if for no other reason—we must ourselves stand somewhere. We must assert some sort of ultimate values in the face of heaven-knows-what social, intellectual, moral, and religious pressures—in this case, the values of persons and of their rights, and corresponding to that the value of the free, just, and equal community that this theocratic tyranny so deeply threatens. And to assert our ultimate value or values is to assert a "world," a view of all reality. For each affirmed political, moral, or religious value presupposes a certain understanding of human beings, society, and history, and so a certain understanding of the whole in which they exist. Our view of existence as a whole gives locus in reality to the values we here defend. Consequently, any practical political action—in resistance to tyranny or in liberation from it—presupposes ultimate values and an ultimate vision of things, an ethic and so a theology. And it presupposes an absolute commitment to this understanding of things. This union of resistance, commitment, and "world" was made crystal clear by the Barman Confession: to confess our adherence to one Lord is at once to resist the Nazi claim on our allegiance; conversely to resist Nazi ideology, allegiance alone to one Lord and to one Word was required. The necessity of action, liberating action, calls first for the relinquishment of all relativity and second for the assertion of some alternative absolute standpoint. Paradoxically, plurality, precisely by its own ambiguity, implies both relativity and absoluteness, a juxtaposition or synthesis of the relative and the absolute that is frustrating intellectually and yet necessary practically.

A Dialectical Wager: A Relative Absoluteness

We have seen the theoretical dilemma plurality has forced upon us. On the one hand, the inescapable drive toward ecumenical community, toward respect for and recognition of the other as other, and of the religious validity and power he or she embodies has pushed us toward a relativity that seems to defy intellectual resolution. There seems no consistent theological way to relativize and yet to assert our own symbols. And yet we must do both in dialogue. On the other hand, the shadow side of religious plurality frequently forces us to resist, to stand somewhere, and to hold some alternative religious position with absolute fidelity, courage, and perseverance. How are we to understand and resolve this contradiction or puzzle dealt us by plurality?

Faced with this reflective impasse, I suggest we refer to the venerable, practical American tradition. The puzzle, which to *reflection* may represent a hopeless contradiction, said John Dewey, can through *intelligent practice* be fruitfully entered and successfully resolved. As William James reminds us, moreover, praxis brings with it a *forced* option, one that cannot be avoided. When praxis is called for, both the puzzled immobility before a contradiction and the indifferent acceptance of a plurality of options must cease. For to be humanly existing, we must wager—and must enact our wager. So is it with the dilemma forced on us by an oppressive ideology: faced with that menace, we *must* act; we *will* act whether we wish to or not. More specifically, we will *either* conform, *or* we will resist. Both are actions, choices that transform much about ourselves that went before, not least our relation to our social environment. Praxis and its demands do not leave us alone. Thus does praxis push as well as lure us into the heart of our puzzle.

That puzzle has revealed itself as the apparent contradiction between the requirement within political action for some fixed or absolute center and an equally unavoidable relativism. Let us look first at this requirement or center for praxis and then see how it also relativizes itself if it is to remain healthy. If we would *be* as personal and social beings, and even more if we must take a role in liberating action, we must stand somewhere and act from somewhere. We need a ground for the apprehension and understanding of reality that undergirds our choices, our critiques of the status quo, our policies. We need a ground for the values and eros that fuel and drive toward justice, and for our criteria for the judgments essential both for reflective construction and for liberating doing. And we need priorities in value if we would creatively and actively move into the future. All this is as true of the pragmatic humanist as it is of the theologian, and for the reflection and action of each.

There seems to appear here as a requirement of authentic being a relation on the one hand to some stable and assumed and, in that sense, *absolute* standpoint, a participation in it, and commitment to it. But on the other hand (and here is where the polar side of the dialectic appears), to avoid repeating in ourselves the same oppressive religious absolutism that we confront, there must at the same time be a deep apprehension and recognition of the *relativity* of our standpoint. A dialectic or paradox combining and interweaving both one part absoluteness and two parts relativity, *a relative absoluteness*, represents a posture essential to public and political praxis, again whether humanistic or theological.

With regard to praxis in the other larger area of plurality, namely, the new interrelations of religions to one another, the same dialectic or paradox—this interweaving and mutual dependence of apparent opposites appears. As we have seen, in the face of parity of religions, it is almost impossible at the moment to formulate a theological resolution of the doctrinal dilemmas and contradictions involved. For the interplay of absolute and relative—of being a Christian, Jew, or Buddhist and *affirming* that stance, and yet at the same time relativizing that mode of existence—both stuns and silences the mind, at least mine. But again praxis, now in the form of dialogue between diverse positions, pushes and lures us into the middle of a maze we still can hardly enter intellectually. As we do creative political action, so now in "doing dialogue" we embody and enact this paradox. And we do so most fruitfully step by step. On the one hand we do not relinquish our own standpoint or starting point: what is the dialogue if our Buddhist partner ceases to be Buddhist or we cease to be Christian? Nor on the other hand do we absolutize our own standpoint, lest no interchange take place at all. On the contrary, we relativize it radically. Truth and grace are *also* with the other, so that now ours is no longer the *only* way. And yet we remain *there*, embodying stubbornly but relatively our unconditional affirmations. Or, in reverse, we qualify our acknowledged relativism by participating in our quite particular but still stoutly affirmed perspective. Again, in praxis we uncover a *relative absoluteness.*

What to reflection is a contradiction is to praxis a workable dialectic, a momentary but creative paradox. Absolute and relative, unified vision and plurality, a centered principle of interpretation and mere difference, represent polarities apparently able to be embodied in crucial practice despite the fact that they seem numbing in reflective theory. Thus reflection must not, because it cannot, precede praxis; on the contrary, it must be begun on the basis of praxis. The basic principle of such theory based on praxis is that what is necessary to praxis is also necessary for reflection and theory—though the reverse is not true.

Nevertheless, reflection is important and must be begun. Let us, therefore, start our reflections with this dialectic or paradox uncovered as the heart of praxis in relation to plurality, namely, political liberation and dialogue. And let us then push it reflectively outward toward theory, toward theology. I suggest we use this paradigm within praxis—the dialectic of infinity and the finite, of the absolute as *relatively* present in the relative as the clue to the center of theological understanding—to the interpretation of our relation to the sacred on the one hand (our religion) and on the other as the key to reflection on that to which we are related—to the absolute as it manifests itself relatively in the relative, to "God." Recall that the structure of praxis is our most helpful clue to the structure of being as we now seek to reflect on it.

The infinite manifests itself in the particular, the absolute in the relative, and the aroma of *each* pervades all we do
and think. Is this principle or insight new? Is it not the heart of
Hegel, even of Kierkegaard? Is it not what Whitehead meant
when he speaks of an infinite mystery hovering over and relativizing any system of rational coherence? Or what Dewey
pointed to when amid perpetual flux and relativity he lifted up
a method that was not relative and did not change? Or what
Tillich pointed to with his concept of the *true* symbol that relativizes and sacrifices itself in pointing beyond itself? Or
Niebuhr, who orchestrated the theme of a mystery deeper than
any revealed or reflected scheme? What is different, what is
more radical, in our situation than in these classical texts?
Each of these saw clearly the dialectic of infinity and manifestation, of absolute and relative, of unconditioned mystery and
meaning. The difference is that each, true to their cultural and
religious epoch, saw its own particularity, its concrete scheme
of meaning, be it theological or philosophical, as somehow
privileged, as final, as less relative than the others, as *the* clue
to the mystery that transcends it—whether it was Hegel's or
Whitehead's logos, Dewey's expanded scientific method, or
Tillich's and Niebuhr's revelation. But an objective and universal rational order turns out to be a *Western* logos, and this for
us defies the awareness of the plurality and relativity of cultures, and so of all logoi. And the claim to a final and definitive
revelation defies the plurality and relativity of religions. No cultural logos is final and universal (even one based on science);
no one revelation is or can be the universal criterion for all the
others (even one based on Christian revelation, as we are now
seeing). Mystery is here more encompassing because the particular center, the concrete principle of meaning, is now *in itself*
relative, one among other centers. This is the new situation, and
again it seems to stifle any philosophy grounded on a universal
logos or any theology on a universally valid revelation.

So we shall return to our dialectic incarnate in unavoidable praxis: the infinite manifests itself in *relative* relativities, the unconditioned in *conditioned* concretions. Liberating theologies and dialogue are based on this. But can we *think* as well as act on this new basis? Let us turn this over. These manifestations are particular and relative, agreed. But despite this, they also participate in and manifest the absolute or the infinite. The infinite *is* in the concrete. The absolute is unavoidably in the particular; it cannot be approached except through the particular and the relative. But, therefore, the particular and the relative are not completely relative, for neither praxis nor reflection can be without the absolute ground and meaning. A symbol or a criterion points beyond itself and criticizes itself if it would not be demonic. But it also points *to* itself and *through* itself if it would not be empty, and if we would not be left centerless. The dialectic works *both* ways: relativizing the manifestations on the one hand, and so all incarnations of the absolute, yet manifesting as well *through* the relative an absoluteness that transcends it, else again there be no liberating praxis and no creative reflection possible. I suspect our wider culture, and also the academy, will soon—but by no means yet—have to deal with this same dilemma: the relativism and yet the continued affirmation of Western forms of scientific, historical, and social consciousness—as the American Medical Association (AMA) is having to deal with acupuncture, and Detroit with Toyota! We are now in the very middle of this in theology. How are we to understand Christian revelation and promise as our affirmed ground of life, of political praxis and reflection, but as *relative*—as one among other manifestations and grounds?

We must, then, not be ashamed to start with our particularity, our relativity—for no universal standpoint, cultural or religious, is readily available to us. But we must incorporate into the theological elaboration of these particular symbols a new and pervasive realization and expression of their relativity, a new and deeper "speaking and not speaking" at once. Thus I will attempt to give this dialectic or paradox of infinity and manifestation, of absolute and relative, one of its *Christian* or particular forms as at the moment the best I can do. For as any vision of plurality is itself qualified by the affirmation of a relative center, so each apprehension of infinite meaning is qualified by and expressed through particular symbols.

In Christian symbols—as in the historical events that were their occasion and inspiration—there is a *relative* manifestation of *absolute* meaning. They are true and yet relatively true; they represent a particularization of the absolute, and yet are relative and therefore only one manifestation. The relative here participates in and manifests the absolute; thus, as relative, it negates and transcends itself. It is final and yet not the only one; it is definitive and yet so are other ways. These are paradoxical assertions. Are these paradoxes contradictory so that they cancel each other out? Or are they strange windows to an even stronger mystery, and keys or clues to renewed theology? If the latter, then they represent challenges to what are in that case conventional but false dichotomies: (1) The absolute is lost if its relative expression becomes relative. In answer, possibly relativity and absoluteness could in reflection, as they do in praxis, coexist. (2) The relative loses all participation in and communication of the absolute if it is relative to others, if there *are* others. In answer again, possibly a series of manifestations can coexist on the same level and with genuine validity. At least it is this that seems to me now existentially and theologically possible as it is in any sane, liberating, and humane praxis.

Thus, to mention briefly a further theological elaboration of this fundamental dialectic: (1) The infinite can be seen as God—and yet that symbol recognized as transcended by an infinite mystery, a mystery consequently pervaded by nonbeing as well as being (as the cross might remind us), and so a mystery truly but relatively manifest as God but also made particular and concrete in other ways and through other symbols. (2) Correspondingly, the infinite is revealed christologically as absolute love, as agape. Here is a truth, yet a truth whose vehicle of manifestation whereby it is known and apprehended is relative, and yet true. What is here truly apprehended, acknowledged, and witnessed to may be also expressed through other media and by means of other symbols (for example, the bodhisattva). (3) The infinite mystery is, finally, understood as redemptive power and promise, and truly so understood. Yet the grace there known far transcends the bounds of its own manifestations. To understand God in relation both to a mystery that transcends God and to the nonbeing that seems to contradict God; to understand revelation in relation to other revelations that relativize our revelations; to view Christology and gospel in relation to other manifestations of grace; to view anthropology in relation to the "no soul" (anatta) doctrine of Buddhism and the emphasis on identity in Christianity—this is the heart of our present baffling but very exciting theological task.

Perhaps the secret here is like the secret of existing itself: existing with inner strength and outer liberating power—holding on with infinite passion to both ends of the dialectic of relativity and absoluteness. Perhaps, if one keeps these poles together in a synthesis, such a posture for theological reflection may seem possible, as it is already acknowledged to be possible in political action and in dialogue. If such a relativized theology seems, as it certainly will to its cultural critics, a foolish and illogical impossibility, then let them remember that they will face tomorrow the same baffling dialectic as the Western consciousness appropriates to itself its own destined travail of relativity. Meanwhile, let us not forget that the present flood of relativity is balanced by the stern demands for liberating praxis and for creative theory.

11

the religious situation
at the beginning of the new millennium

Our theme, the religious situation, has been made difficult because of Paul Tillich's splendid long essay of 1926; we cannot hope to duplicate that magnificent analysis. But then we could not duplicate it anyway; we do not have the insight, and our situation is too different, both from a century ago and from the time he lived and wrote. Still, as always, what he had to say is surprisingly relevant to our very different cultural and historical circumstances. My aim will be to point out that relevance in relation to four issues, all of them appearing within the last half century, that, it seems to me, dominate our religious situation. None of these will surprise most readers. Nonetheless, what Tillich had to say about each of them in another form—and what he might have said about them now—is significant.

Religious Pluralism

The first issue that characterizes our current religious situation is the challenge of religious pluralism—the appearance in the last four decades of the many religions in what we have called "rough parity" with one another and especially with a formerly all-powerful West and its Christianity. The result has been the sprouting of dialogue between the representatives of the many religions—an instructive and exciting activity in which, I suspect, most of us have been involved. It is not hard to carry on

dialogue, if one obeys the useful rules of respectful listening
and of refraining from heavy apologetics—the rules, as Jim
Wiggins put it, of courteous conversation. But it is very hard—
at least I have found it so—to know *theologically* what one is
doing and above all how one is to comprehend *theologically* the
ambiguity of one's own position in the act of dialogue. Tillich
was, I believe, the one theologian of his generation who, toward
the end of his life and especially after his trip to Japan, felt
powerfully the immense significance of the new situation. This
situation had been brought on, I think, by the collapse of the
European empires at the end of World War II and the relative
autonomy which that disappearance of colonialism in Asia,
India, the Islamic lands, and Africa gave to non-European cultures and religions. By the early 1960s, Tillich was pondering
this new situation deeply and radically; however, we do not
know with any accuracy what he would have said.

        Nonetheless, I think he would have declared what many
of us have since concluded, namely, that there is no objective,
universal position from which to approach other religions. One
may, as many who termed themselves pluralists sought to do,
attempt to abstract oneself from one's own religious tradition
and its assumptions. But then one seems inescapably to find
oneself, along with John Hick, in a Western-type ethical
monotheism, or with Paul Knitter, in a liberationist theological
stance—each one worthy enough, to be sure, but perhaps even
less universal than, say, Buddhism, as Abe Masao has been
quick to point out. For Tillich, there is no escape from the theological circle; one thinks as one acts from participating in one's
cultural and historical milieu, out of one's deepest religious
substance, whether one is doing ontology or theology. As in the
case of morals, reason is finite and so perspectival, and in each
of us, both morality and reason are cramped and even warped
by estrangement. As Tillich said, logos has a fate and is ever
subject to its *kairos.* In this sense, we are all, whether we like
it or not, inclusivists. Here Tillich reflects his neoorthodox

contemporaries' sense of the relativity of all things historical and cultural, as well as much in present postmodernism.

The only resolution of this dilemma of the infinity of spirit and the fatedness of finite reason is, he said, dialectical and existential. And here the appearance of the New Being provides us with the clue to the only path to the universal, though there are many earlier forms of this point, for example, in the "No" of prophetic religion to itself (*Basic Principles of Religious Socialism* [1923], found in James Luther Adams, ed., *Political Expectation* [New York: Harper & Row, 1971] 65). The true symbol, says Tillich, true of the universality of the divine ground, is one that, though remaining in continuity with its ground, nonetheless points away from and beyond itself to its ultimate source and ground: here there is "complete transparency and complete self-sacrifice" (Paul Tillich, *Systematic Theology*, vol. 1 [Chicago: University of Chicago Press, 1951–63] 151); in the true symbol, there is "uninterrupted unity with the ground of his being and the continual sacrifice of himself" (*Systematic Theology*, vol. 1, 137). The only valid universality is that which points beyond itself and sacrifices itself and its concreteness—even its historical concreteness—to a universal beyond itself.

Perhaps this can be a clue to the resolution of the new problem of pluralism: the sacrifice not only of Jesus to the Christ, as Tillich had put it, but even the sacrifice of the absoluteness of the latter, even of the tradition itself, to the ultimate mystery of being and of nonbeing. It is at least a thought, a Tillichian thought.

Nature

The second issue arising during and just after Tillich's last years is the issue of nature or our exploitation of nature. As a consequence, a new theological concentration on nature, a theology of nature emerged—an issue that has gradually come to dominate all our minds since Rachel Carson's *Silent Spring* of

the early 1960s. As with the first issue, Tillich did not live to
develop a theology of nature. But he had, I think, many helpful
things to say to those of us who have had to try.

First, however, let me recount an amusing incident on
this topic that occurred when Tillich came to Vanderbilt to give
the Cole Lectures in the late 1950s. In April, middle Tennessee
is ablaze with glorious trees and flowers, and I was determined
to show Tillich the pick of Nashville's gardens, culminating in
some uncut property I had discovered in the hills to the south
of the city. After all, in those neoorthodox days, he was the only
theologian one could possibly have called a "nature mystic."
Did he not talk ecstatically about gazing out over the sea and
feeling its unconditioned power and sacrality (Paul Tillich,
"On the Boundary, Between City and Country," in *The Interpretation of History*. Trans. N. A. Rasetzke [New York: Charles
Scribner's Sons, 1936) 7–8)? We drove up some low hills on a
tiny dirt road, and I hopped out of the car. Stretching below us
was a long meadow of high grass, covered with dogwood, red-
bud, and rhododendron, and then rising up to a hilltop. I said
eagerly, "Let's go walking, Paulus!" He stood there nervously
staring straight ahead: "Are zer serpents here, Langdon?" Note,
he did not say "snakes," a merely secular beast! "Yes," I said
heedlessly, "There are some few rattlers in these hills, but they
never bother us if we take care." "Zen I get back in ze car." "But
Paulus, don't you want to see the glories of uncut nature?" "No,
Langdon. I am a zity boy, and I get back in ze car!"—so much,
I thought, in surprise and amusement, for the nature mystic!

Still, Tillich had some very interesting things to say to
those of us trying to think theologically about nature. First of
all, his radical reworking of the symbol of estrangement—
estrangement is "sin," he said, but he preferred the word *estrangement*—clarifies infinitely the destructive exploitation
with which modern culture has threatened the being of nature.
Central to estrangement, he said—and here he was almost
alone in his generation—is concupiscence and, as with all those

old words, Tillich gives it a new (though there are hints in Augustine) and very relevant meaning. Concupiscence, he says, is the desire of the finite—now alone among finitude—for infinity, but *through* grasping only the finite. Thus it is a craving for the entire world, to possess and dominate it. As he remarked once: "The attempt to cram the whole world into one's mouth," "to attain and devour unlimited abundance." This represents, I think, a very powerful model of the essential sin of a consumer, goods society: an endless and ruthless drive or desire to possess and enjoy everything, an urge that uses persons, objects, and materials endlessly—and then casts them off, leaving behind a desert of destruction and no hint of satiety. The consequence of this sin inwardly is an utter emptiness of soul, with no real relations or vocation in life. And objectively it means, granted the technical power to do so, the ultimate destruction of nature. Tillich here, alone among his generation, has uncovered the form of sin that has led our civilization to the crisis of ecology.

Tillich does not develop his philosophical base thoroughly; one wishes he had written and defended the epistemology and ontology he uses to get as quickly as he can to theology. But he initiates in volume 3 of *Systematic Theology* a most interesting and relevant epistemology to which it is not inaccurate to apply the term *critical realism.* For me, it points the way to understanding how we might be able to know the world and not destroy it. There is no self without a world, says Tillich, but equally, there is no world—no ordered, named, and comprehended cosmos—without a self to name and organize it. Thus language and technology express a union with the world as well as a separation from it, a union in which both object and subject (objective and subjective logos) participate and to which therefore both contribute. As a result, the world in itself is not as directly and unequivocally known by our inquiries as we assume, and hence nature is in itself much more mysterious, rich, and creative than are the named objects that we know and can manipulate. In knowing the world, reason must participate in the world as well as survey and investigate it: cosmos and consciousness are interdependent, and they unite in their common ground. Otherwise, without participating in the world it knows, reason leads to "controlling reason," which, driven as we saw by concupiscence, leaves behind it only a ruined world and a vulnerable self. Like the epistemology of Whitehead, which is in many surprising ways similar, this is a remarkably prophetic epistemology, written long before the ecological crisis. If further developed, it may help us to understand and possibly surmount this deep crisis.

Radical Heteronomy

The third issue, I am sure, has occurred to Tillichians long since as a most illuminating confirmation of the master's genius in seeing into the inner dynamics of a complex social and religious situation. This is the new appearance in our time of the threat of a radical heteronomy, embodied in the quite unexpected growth in the religious, social, and political power of the Religious Right. Tillich would not have been surprised that this has arisen out of its dialectical opposite, namely, an unraveling autonomy, an autonomy that, on several important points, has—to use Tillich's words—devolved from an originally theonomous situation into one of increasing profanization. This unraveling has apparently for many left life, ordinary life, desacralized and hence bereft of ultimate meanings—in short, as he described it, empty and so open for the radical return of its lost sacred content, namely, heteronomy. Tillich described this unraveling process in his religious socialist writings of the 1920s, and thus he understood it largely in terms of the dynamics of the confused postwar society he then faced. Obviously our situation differs on many scores. Yet, as is evident, the characteristics of a profanized autonomy calling for a semidemonic heteronomy are clearly similar. Let us see, therefore, if we can give a Tillichian analysis of what has led to the present power and threat of the Religious Right.

Tillich defined theonomy in 1923 as "a condition in which the spiritual and social forms are filled with the import of the Unconditioned as the foundation, meaning and reality of all forms," and again "the unity of sacred form and sacred import in a concrete historical situation" (*Basic Principles of Religious Socialism*, in *Political Expectation*, 62). We note that this definition makes no reference to churches, to religious communities, or to "religion" as such; it concerns solely vocations in the social and cultural spheres. His point is that under the pressure of a waxing autonomy, this theonomous unity unravels, or, better put, a secular, self-sufficient autonomy dissipates this sacred import, leaving the social forms or vocations empty and meaningless, and as a result creating vast anxiety and restlessness. The need for the sacred remains—the need for ultimate concern, unconditional meaning or, as he frequently says, unconditional seriousness in what we are and do. As he remarks in *The Religious Situation* (Trans. H. Richard Niebuhr [New York: Henry Holt & Co., 1932] 35): "to live spiritually is to live in the presence of meaning, and without an ultimate meaning everything disappears into the abyss of meaninglessness." To rescue the lost meanings from this abyss the sacred returns, but now not confidently and creatively *in* and *through* the autonomous forms as in theonomy, where the import of ultimate meaning represents the growing religious substance of the culture. Instead it returns *over against* these now profanized autonomous forms, controlling them, reshaping them, and if necessary crushing them—as surely the Religious Right would wish, if it could, to do. This is the abstract process as Tillich describes it, which is valid, as he says, for any number of historical situations. Now we will look at our own recent situation to see how this process has worked its way out there.

Let us begin where I think the Religious Right would begin, namely, with what is to them the loss of all moral standards: "the amoral mass of American society," as William

Bennett termed it, surveying the recent public refusal to im-
peach the president. And in a strange sense he is right; there has
been immense slippage, so to speak, of the authority of older, established moral rules in our society whether we speak of sexual
mores, public and private, through permissive parents who find
themselves bereft of parental authority, to drugs and alcohol, to
explicit violence, explicit language, and explicit sex. We each
have our likes and our dislikes in this list, and the list could go
on and on. We probably do not feel the full weight of all this—
only the new freedom to choose what we wish to choose in a
much wider area. But as Tillich reminds us, this new freedom is
the luxury of an upper middle, professional class, used to being
in charge of their important decisions. It is not necessarily a
complete freeing for everyone. In such a permissive culture,
many who are now bereft of what are to them traditional rules
and criteria find themselves lost or adrift—or see their spouses
or their children to be so. In this situation, the reappearance of
strict, even authoritarian, rules can seem to perform a needed
reshaping of a shapeless life and so a genuine rescue operation.
And to such persons, adherence to unyielding principles based
on belief is better than the appearance of adherence based on
conformity. As our worthy friend Henry Hyde said of his fellow
prosecutors: "At least we believed in *something!*"

Lest, however, we too become sentimental over a lost
morality, let us recall that these same traditional rules in America in many ways thoroughly deserved their fate. They reflected
authoritarian patterns of a patriarchal, hence male-dominated,
society; they leaned sharply in the direction of white supremacy;
they reflected a wildly exaggerated notion of property—and, of
course, of guns. And like much that came to us out of the last
century, they did not encourage a genuine and creative autonomy or diversity. Thus, for good or for ill, the twentieth century
has had to spend much of its time and energy, beginning in the
1920s, through the 1930s and 1940s—skip the 1950s—and
into its later decades, steadily and on *moral* grounds dispensing

with these older moral codes and rules. This is, I am suggesting, one of the reasons we have reached our present situation, with its very noticeable moral and especially fundamentalist reaction, a reaction that took us all, confused but relatively autonomous, middle-class professionals, completely by surprise.

This unraveling of older moral certainties was, therefore, a *moral* event carried out by moral conscience, an event that has made our country a *more* moral place—as was the dissolution of the empires in the middle of the twentieth century. But that unraveling—like the dissolution of empires—bears with it also a fairly heavy bill to be paid *somewhere*—and this is Tillich's point. In this case, the bill is present in the vast anxiety of those who depended on the sacramental consecration of males and of whites in traditional America. As Tillich notes, a similar bill had to be paid in Europe for the dissipation of the sacrality of class, status, place, and "blood" after World War I. In our time, the phrase "Make love and not war" appealed to most of us here, and still does. But it almost certainly horrified and terrified much of traditional America, and the onset of heteronomy is one result of that terror, as it was in the 1920s and 1930s in Germany.

While we are on this point, one of Tillich's most suggestive insights concerned what we have just called, as he did, "sacramental consecration," and in places "sacramental demonries." In traditional societies, Tillich pointed out, authority—and therefore social and political power—is sacramental: the presence in certain groups, inevitably ruling groups (for example, the European nobility), of a seemingly holy power, which gives them unapproachable splendor and unchallengeable authority. Rational bourgeois consciousness and religious socialism alike rejected this traditional class and blood "sacramental demonry," said Tillich. And they rejected it in the name of *justice.* The reason justice called for this rejection was that others not included in these charmed circles were unable to become free personalities, autonomous, self-directing, self-affirming, and respected.

Tillich is, I am sure, absolutely right about this. I suspect that much of what he called the power of origins that had dissolved in his youth in Germany has in our time and place undergone a like experience, namely, the dissolution of similar "sacramental consecrations" in traditional America. I refer here to the challenge that came in the last half century to the "sacramental consecration" of male, of white, and of propertied, "hard-working" citizens. All of these had assumed as a birthright the presence in ourselves of this sacrality, a sacramental consecration given to white persons, and among them especially to males, and not given to others. The loss, stolen as if at night, of this sacrality, and the assumed authority and power that go with it, is more than baffling; it can be terrifying. Out of this anxiety, too, can come the need for a new heteronomy to bring the sacred back—as the Southern Baptists recently showed us with their bizarre and foolish statements about marriage! Tillich here, I think, gives us some very helpful hints about theologies of liberation. Final liberation, he seems to say, does not come merely with equal access to jobs, rewards, political power, or social prominence; it must finally come from a *just* dissolution of the sacramental consecration of formerly ruling groups.

We return to our theme of theonomy, autonomy, and heteronomy. The most comprehensive definition of theonomy, and so of its opposite, an unraveling autonomy, concerns the possibility and the reality of ultimate concerns, "an unconditional seriousness" about our vocations and our lives because the latter are felt to contain an unconditional, if finite and partial, meaning or import. As Tillich very perceptively notes, Americans have long received the courage to be—and so the courage to face potential and actual suffering, loss, and death—largely through their participation in a progressive productive process (*The Courage to Be* [New York: Yale University Press, 1952] 109–11). This participation, he further notes, demands conformity and adjustment, but it gives to life immense courage even in the face of possible failure. In participation in this progressive productive process (for example, even in theology), lie I suspect for many of us the grounds for whatever courage to be as an individual or as a part we may have had, and so the basis for much of the sense of ultimate worth of what we are and do. My point is that the sense of "building America"—or, if we prefer, of furthering our enterprise or profession, or even building our town—has dissipated along with the more abstract belief in progress. That abstract belief was ruthlessly battered by the theologians of Tillich's generation; it is now rejected, I take it, even more repeatedly by postmodernism. But here I refer to widespread feelings and assumptions, not intellectual ideas. And here what was once a serene confidence has disintegrated into anxiety about the economic future, about whether growth is really good, and a host of other factors.

I am suggesting that the location of the ultimate concern of each of us up and down the social scale in the creative, progressive process has in our time become increasingly elusive. The loss of the sense of creative progress has left people alone in the complex process with no universal ground, no confidence beyond itself, no place to do its small work and feel worthy. It has, therefore, been replaced in much of society by something much more worldly, secular, profane, and less empowering: the explicit drive to get ahead, to gain power or fame, and especially money. This, as we noted, Tillich called *concupiscence*, and the Buddhists call *desire*. Tillich earlier termed it "irrational forces, power and eros, the infinite drive to dominate," and later it represented to him the main face of sin in a commercial, goods culture. We are reminded of his very early criticism of a capitalist society as one driven by "the limitless rational will to power . . . leading to an endless conflict of all against all" (*Basic Principles of Religious Socialism*, in *Political Expectation*, 76–77). In a world driven by concupiscence, there are no ultimate concerns, only desires for things and power. There is no self, there are no persons, and there is no world, only objects to be used and discarded. Hence there is neither worth nor meaning that can alone come with real relations to persons and a serious vocation in the world. If this is so, then that emptiness could itself call for a return of the sacred, a holy call to work not just for ourselves but also for the Lord—a cry commonly heard among the Religious Right. The irony is (considering Tillich's distaste for capitalism) that this is a cry of the Religious Right, one of whose most ultimate of ultimate concerns is the preservation of a radically individualistic capitalism!

Other analyses, probably much more informed and accurate, could be made of our present religious situation and its obvious yearning for an authoritarian, fundamentalist religion, a genuine heteronomy. I have found it, however, personally very illuminating to apply to our own dilemmas Tillich's insights about those of his own time.

Space

We cannot consider the passage to a new century without confronting its most immediate problem: ethnic cleansing and the hordes and hordes of refugees, battered, raped, murdered, and in the end driven out of their own space to a place they know not where. There are many more important things to say about this tragic situation. But each time I encounter it, I think of what Tillich said about *space*, for his comments showed a vast sensitivity on his part to the deep anxiety and terror of being a refugee.

Each being, he said, needs a space, as well as a present in time, in order to be. This space is both physical—a place, a home, a community, a country—and social—a group or circle, a vocation, a role. Not to have a space is not to be. But no finite being *possesses* a space; each being is at best *lent* its space. Thus it can be removed from its space, and ultimately it will be. As Tillich reminds us: "Its place knoweth it no more." Finitude, therefore, is *essentially* insecure, both in time and in space, and we are all inwardly, if hiddenly, aware of that. Hence there exists a deep and abiding anxiety about space, signaled by the immense importance of the latch, the door, the fence, the border. These have been ultimate concerns of almost infinite historical weight (*Systematic Theology*, vol. 1, 194–95). Refugees who are herded out of their space and sent into no space undergo, therefore, extreme suffering, not only of hunger, cold, abuse, and death, but also the deep terror of spacelessness.

When I heard Tillich speak with real seriousness of this in class in 1947, I recalled at once the European Jewish family I saw in that restaurant in Yokohama, which I described in chapter 7. I felt the terror of this for them then; it could be seen in their eyes, but I did not understand what it was I was feeling. In Tillich's class, at last I understood in part—but only in part—those pale, anxious faces. I think of this terror of spacelessness often these days.

One final word. I had originally titled this chapter "The Religious Situation at the End of the Century" and I want to explain why. I may be quite wrong here, but I decided that to celebrate the millennium might be a little un-Tillichian. The millennium is a matter of numbers, of counting, even if the numbers are impressive. And, as we know, this counting has only a probable, perhaps even an improbable, beginning point in the supposed year one. It is thus in Tillich's terms an issue of "technical reason." It is a matter of abstract numbers and of mere probability, not of qualitative history. Its unfolding, for a Tillichian, represents, therefore, only a matter at best of preliminary concern, and there is for each of us very little of participatory knowing. Tillich, however, *does* have a historical category that refers to qualitative and not quantitative time, that issues into a genuine creativity, and that requires from us a very powerful participation, both of thought and of action.

That is, of course, *kairos*, the appearance of the Eternal in the midst of a concrete historical situation. Thus I would like the present title, even with the use of *millennium* to be understood as "The Religious Situation as We Await with Hope the New *Kairos.*"

12

history and theology

We now want to look at the interweaving, the interdependence, of history and theology—surely one of the central motifs of the Hebrew Scriptures. Hence our first question arises: why should history be understood *theologically*, as well as in a secular, "historical," or "scientific" fashion, as most academics insist? We agree, of course, that history must first be understood "naturalistically"; in terms of all the finite factors, causes, intentions, and actions that bring about events. However, this entire complex set of sequences, we are saying, can be understood only if it also is given as a theological interpretation.

History

History is the history of groups. Nothing becomes historical until it shapes, affects, and characterizes a group and its life. Groups are like the individuals who constitute them, but not exactly. Groups have no organic center, mind, or will. The deliberating and active center of a group is its ruling class, who represent their own interests as well as those of all the others, which is why we take elections so seriously. Nonetheless, groups have analogical traits similar to those of individual humans. They too are self-aware, aware of their own being and security, their possibilities and greatness, their difficulties, threats, and possible death. Since each individual is in large part made secure and given possibilities by his group, the security and well-being of the community represent an ultimate concern for each of us. The group's strength is accordingly our strength, its vulnerability correspondingly our vulnerability, its dangers our dangers. Communities and their history are thus a matter of ultimate concern, of celebration or of fear and terror. History as the expanding of life and possible death of groups exists within a horizon of ultimacy, that is to say, a *religious* horizon.

Groups do have a measured freedom in history—freedom to respond creatively to what is given to them in order to further their own ends. This freedom characterizes some communities more than others, depending on their power. But even the powerful groups, who feel their strength and freedom to control things, are vulnerable. Their power has been given to them by the historical trends, the relations to others, and by the fortuitous events of both the distant and the immediate past, by the "destiny" that has made them what they presently are. Hence that power and freedom can be taken away, as they have been so often in history from even the most powerful of nations. Our control over events is not itself in our control. That control comes to us only if fortune blesses us with the continuing power to control. Hence we too experience the unsettling possibility of fate. Fate is a given or a destiny in which a group is presented with *no* possibilities, no chance of creativity or well-being, no ability to determine its own life. Many groups and classes in our time experience this fatedness. They are dependent on trends beyond their control; they are thus unable to rise, unable to guarantee their own security or power, unable to generate any freedom. Every group is liable to undergo this experience in the turbulence of history, as even all-powerful Rome shows. And as the tremors in the twentieth century in both economic and political life made us all aware, even we, too, are thus vulnerable, perhaps helpless, in relation to historical passage. We sense this, and we know that we must cope with this possibility as best we can.

Government is the handle with which each community seeks to deal with what is given to it and to secure a better future. Government is, therefore, that through which a group gains and preserves its freedom and well-being in history, and hence through which it seeks to stave off fate. Two important consequences follow from this crucial role of government. First, this is why government has always had a *sacred* role in all history: through government, a community deals with implacable fate, a suprahuman task. No wonder politics is steeped in myth. Second, this is the fundamental reason for the fanaticism and infinite cruelty of groups in history. For each community that is involved, this struggle represents an ultimate battle of being and nonbeing, of security and insecurity, of life and death.

Each community also embodies and lives from a definite social structure and a corresponding system of symbols expressive of that structure. Democracy and communism are good examples. These symbol systems not only shape the institutions and life of a society, they also shape the consciousness of their members. They are, moreover, deeply intertwined with the security and well-being of the group. Each bloc in the Cold War was almost as concerned with the commitment of its members to its way of life, to its ideology, as it was with its material power. As a consequence, each of these systems parades before history as ultimate, as absolute. They appear to their adherents as representing the essential grain of all history—as democracy surely still does, as communism once did, and as each political party reiterates as it seeks control. These symbols represent not a relative truth and good, one to be gone tomorrow, but an absolute truth and good. Are freedom and tolerance only relative goods? Is the counting of every vote only a passing fad? Is an authoritarian or a racist government only relatively wrong?

The symbolic structure and the corresponding norms of a group are thus for each group-consciousness ultimate and absolute, essential for the entire grain of history, bearers of truth and good alike. This absolutizing of our own ideology is, moreover, the source of a wide variety of very dubious human traits. For instance, the universality of propaganda in politics—the claim of truth through a lie, the universality of hypocrisy, and the claim of virtue by the self-concerned, witness by their pretensions of truth and virtue to the necessity for each community to possess or represent an ultimate truth and an ultimate good in historical and political life. This ever-present propaganda and hypocrisy were thoroughly illustrated in the 2000 Florida presidential vote recount. As R. W. Apple Jr. of the *New York Times* remarked, "Beneath the noble toga, find naked ambition!"

We must add that despite the presence of propaganda and hypocrisy in all social symbol systems, political rhetoric about its principles and ideals is utterly necessary for any community. Such rhetoric is not just public relations, a veneer of extravagant claims directed at "others." It is essential both for the ruling political agents themselves and for the community that supports them. No community can exist without an awareness and appreciation of the important institutional structures that create its identity; those structures would wither and vanish quickly enough if such awareness ceased. The appeals to these principles and ideals may well, in what theology terms a "fallen" history, have a phony ring—but such appeals must go on. And remember, it is not just politicians that play this game. Every corporation claims to be serving the public, the environment, the hungry; only money-making concerns claim to make money, but always for you and yours!

To return to our theme of absolutism: John Dewey and his many followers rightly saw that the presence of absolutism in social existence was the source of the fury and the intolerance of the political. And they also rightly discerned a religious element in such claims to ultimate truth and virtue. Those of us who recall the absolute claims and the final cruelty of the totalitarian governments in the twentieth century cannot but agree. However, we note that philosophers, historians, and social scientists who have agreed with Dewey, and who wish to banish all absolutism and so all religion from modern culture, have themselves spoken of a "free society" in the same awed and final terms as their grandparents once spoke of a Christian society.

Finally, as with the Old Testament, we all apprehend the presence in our history of sin and, more rarely, of judgment. What happens to us is never just error based on bad luck. Rather, it is always *someone's* fault, someone else's, especially someone else who is our rival. These opponents were not forced to act in as hostile a fashion as they do; on the contrary, they have chosen to do what they did, and so they are to blame. This consciousness of deliberate evil on the part of others permeates history. Each nation and party insists it was necessary for it to do whatever ambiguous act it has grudgingly had to own up to; its opponents, however, are regarded as having freely chosen their dubious deeds—again whether these be statements of the State Department or of a political party. Obviously, the uneasy conscience, although well buried in public affairs, is quite universal. This leads, of course, to the mythical pictures on both sides of the demonic opponent against our own righteous and valiant knight. The much profounder sense of judgment on us all, of course much closer to the truth, is rare indeed in public life, though it characterized the entire prophetic witness. Again, history is inescapably political, and its politics is suffused with a sense of an ultimate evil against our own ultimate good. The concerns of politics are our fundamental being, our security, and our possibilities for the future. Its symbols represent the grain of all history, and the truth and goodness of life itself. However valid the analysis of finite factors in historical change may be, that passage *feels* to the humans immersed within it—even to us—as transpiring within a horizon of the demonic, the sacred, the everlasting, the good, in short a horizon of ultimacy—and thus it requires a theological explication.

Theology

If, then, even in our own day, history must be understood
theologically, how do we so understand it? Our aim is to begin
with the biblical tradition—on which Christian theology is
grounded—and to interpret that tradition in the light of the
way we as moderns understand history. Actually, this approach
is by no means new. Each age has in fact interpreted its sources
in scripture and tradition in the terms of its own understanding
of the world. To us now, this is particularly evident in the case
of the Hellenistic theology of the early church; for us, that theology is throughout shaped by the assumptions of the Greek
and Roman worlds, especially that of later Rome. And this is as
true of the orthodox theology as it is of the so-called heresies of
the period. With liberalism in the early nineteenth century,
shaped as the early liberals were by the new historical consciousness, this method became explicit; we shall, said
Schleiermacher, write theology "for our time." This dependence upon the current view of history even includes Barth,
though he would hardly admit it. His view of history without
the Word is transparently that of the despairing post–World
War I European world: temporal history forms a meaningless
sequence of relative and transitory events rescued only by the
incursion, like a "tangent," of the Word of God—hardly the
view of his spiritual forefather, John Calvin. Thus it is with
what is called the modern historical consciousness, beginning
in the middle of the eighteenth century, that the modern, and
we must add, the postmodern, understanding of history developed. Let us look briefly at this understanding of history to see
where, I believe, most of us in fact are.

There are several important elements to this understanding: the first, and the most radical, is that the fundamental
forms of social and historical life: of family, of government, of
economics, of vocations, and hence also the forms of our understanding of the world and even of our goals and norms,
change as history changes. Both the structure of culture and the

structure of human understanding and willing shift as ages pass. These fundamental social forms were once thought to be changeless, even established by God; now they are seen to be relative to their time and so to shift and pass away. We note that the insight that social or historical forms change preceded the view that biological forms change by almost a hundred years. Second, for the historical consciousness, only *finite* causes are effective in historical life: natural, social, and individual human causes. If, therefore, the divine be active there, God acts only *through* such causes, certainly including our freedom. Third, as a consequence, humans seem immersed in historical time; their modes of consciousness are different from those of other epochs and places. Hence each age is relatively mysterious and obscure to other ages and has difficulty understanding them. There is no universal reason anymore than there are final forms of social life.

Fourth, nonetheless, despite being immersed within history, humans also have the freedom to remake, and so in part to transcend, history. Human intellect and will, human autonomy and freedom, can create the new, that which had not been actual before. The future is thus *open*, a realm of innumerable not-yet possibilities still to be established and made actual by creative human autonomy. Probably the experience of the new science and its technological consequences in the seventeenth and the eighteenth centuries led to this new emphasis on the creativity of freedom. Certainly it led quickly to the theory of cultural progress, to be followed later by the theory of evolutionary progress. The two together dominated the Western consciousness until World War I. The succeeding century has seen that, while knowledge, technology, production, and other social institutions may surely progress, freedom does not progress; waywardness and sin remain. Thus even as civilization ascends, destruction and nemesis may reappear and can bring civilization down. One can well see how the biblical word about betrayal of the covenant followed by nemesis achieved new relevance in the middle half of the twentieth century.

In sum, the modern consciousness has seen history as a thoroughgoing process. All within it is relative, changing, and transient; nothing is absolute, forever, or universal. And yet each moment has the power to add to its past and to create the new. This view has meant a radical temporalizing of historical being: all moves within time from actuality to new possibility. At first, this all-inclusive passage of things was seen as clearly progressive; now we are not sure at all what we see there!

Understanding History and Its Events

We are seeking, then, to interpret the biblical tradition in the light of this new understanding of history and its events. We may note that it has largely been assumed that in such a contingent, relative, and transient history, the conception of God's providence could find no place, that the religious absolute had vanished along with all the other absolutes. How, then, do we, and can we, believe that God is present and active in history so understood?

In reply, let us, with the help of Gerhard von Rad, begin with a look at the biblical understanding. Certainly central to the Old Testament witness is the sovereignty of God in the events of the history through which Israel lived. In the early documents, God was seen as a direct cause of events, but in the later prophetic interpretation, God acts *through* finite events, natural, social, and individual. First of all, God establishes and shapes the institutions and forms of Israel's life, symbolized by the covenant with Israel. Nevertheless, to the prophets, Israel deeply betrays this covenant, and judgment inexorably follows. That is to say, threats of nemesis, suffering, and utter destruction appear as the consequences of betrayal. As Reinhold Niebuhr remarked, Israel through the prophets is far more conscious of its own betrayal of the covenant than the church has ever been of its own faithlessness! Despite these threats of nemesis, however, the prophets declared that there is to be a new creative and redemptive act: the messianic promise to come. Taking, therefore, this witness as our clue to God's role in all of history, we can say that God's actions are here dialectical. First, the divine establishment through human intelligence and will of the traditional structures and norms of community life. Then the human betrayal of these structures and of the covenant embodied in them, and as a result the threat of nemesis: of violence, injustice, destruction, and the suffering that follows. But then, finally, there remains the promise of new creative possibilities to come. When one looks at this dialectical action, one cannot but think on the American covenant in the eighteenth and nineteenth centuries, and of our continual betrayal of it!

As we noted at the beginning, this understanding is not unlike our own experience of historical change when we look closely. The biblical model fits our experience if we can wipe away the myths about historical progress, about good guys and bad guys, and about civilized virtues and backward corruption—again, Florida should divest us of these illusions! We experience our history as having been constituted by human creativity under the guidance of treasured ideals and norms. As a consequence, history is characterized for us by important and value-filled institutions, from which we draw much of the worth of our common life. There seem, therefore, to be endless possibilities for human betterment. These values—of democracy, autonomy, equality, and possibility—represent ultimate concerns for us, as the rhetoric of both Democrats and Republicans in Florida amply shows. We are here dealing with sacred matters.

On the other hand, we also—and daily—experience our betrayal of these ideals, and thus a betrayal of the requirements of these forms of life and of these treasured norms. Despite our denials, we exhibit driving self-interest and the grasp for dominance: proclaiming only our ideals, nonetheless relentlessly we push our interests. Each side, of course, regularly blames the other. But, as in Europe's wars in the last century, and as in Yugoslavia recently, the catastrophes that ensue are judgments on our common past and on the present actions of all of us.

The biblical Word and our experience seem to agree; none are righteous, no, not one—though all deny this and will point their fingers at their opponents. History, therefore, cannot begin to be understood without the thesis of the universality of sin. Of course, there are in all historical circumstances differences, crucial differences between which we must choose; nonetheless, all are tainted with overriding self-concern and hypocrisy. The sense of judgment thus hangs heavily over history whenever catastrophe is looming; an uneasy conscience is what leads each side to deny its involvement and to blame the other. Another helpful biblical clue is that among all the claimants to selfless virtue, and amid, nevertheless, all the evidence of driving self-interest on all sides, one should keep one's eye especially on the *mighty*, the rich, the powerful, the wise and, perhaps especially, the good—for their power and eminence mean that their sins have more destructive effect on others and on the community than do the feebler and less effective sins of the unprivileged.

Like the prophets, moreover, we have experienced new creative acts in our history arising out of destruction and suffering. Hence, however despairing the present situation may be, there is always the continuing possibility of a new chance to come. No political act must but assume this possibility of what presently seems impossible. That confidence is confidence in what is now unseen. It is, as hope always is, the sign of a hidden awareness of providence.

In sum, we experience history as transpiring within a horizon of the sacred, as characterized by a dimension of ultimacy—even though our age seeks to understand all things naturalistically. Historical passage is shaped and grounded by institutions and by forms of social life and values that we regard as ultimate or absolute and for which we know we would give up everything else. Yet we know, too, that we also betray these ideals in every turn of our life. Thus are the mess and the suffering that we encounter daily: at home, at work, in the community, and in the world, also *our* responsibility. And we feel, though we hardly admit it, the heavy hand of judgment. Nonetheless, we look forward to new possibilities given to us by the future. If, therefore, we can remove our illusions about history and about ourselves, we can see the congruence between the prophetic view of history and the reality of the historical world around us—and to help us see this, let me repeat, is the role of theology in our common life.

Finally, allow me to note some of the new elements in the conception of God suggested by this view of divine action in history. The basic understanding for which I have argued is of God in history as the Creator and Preserver of our continuing being in time and of the forms of life as they arise; as the judge on our continuing sin; and as the re-creator of new possibilities. These traits have, to be sure, a traditional ring, as they should do. However, there remain two significant differences from the traditional view.

First, the Creator God is here self-limiting, making room for our freedom. In short, God does not ordain what we do, and so the evil we also do. Nevertheless, God preserves the vanishing past, bringing that past, now gone, into the present as the ground of the present. God also establishes the autonomy and freedom with which we act on that given inheritance. Our freedom is determined neither by the past nor by the impinging future, and surely we do not create it. In this creative role, as preserver of the past and as ground of our freedom in the present, God is unconditioned by anything else, and so here God is above time, timeless, the unconditioned source of the past and of our freedom in the present. But God does not choose what we choose. Thus, as Kierkegaard said, God "steps back" to make room for our choices.

Second, God is temporal and changing. Because the future is open, future possibilities remain only possible until they are made actual in events. The future is not yet there, or it is there only as possibility. Our freedom is a co-creator with God of what each of us does. Thus possibility is only possible until it happens. Before they happen, possibilities are only possible, even for God. When time unfolds, therefore, God changes as these events become actual. God, therefore, *becomes*. But as the ground of the movement of the past into the present, and as the ground of present freedom as well as of the possibilities of the future, God is above time and change as their source, and yet God is also deeply within time.

Let us note that thus God appears *within* and *through* our temporality, our contingency, our relativity, and our freedom—not, as in much of the tradition and as the secular interpreters of history insist, against or in denial of them. In this sense, a theological interpretation of God's action in history accords with our own deepest and contemporary sense of historical passage as relative, radically temporal, and yet shaped by freedom. In fact, such a religious interpretation is essential in order to understand correctly what it is to be human in time.

13

reflections on mortality

Reflection on death has always been a central motif in our Christian tradition. How are we to understand it? What is its cause in God's good creation? Above all, how are we to face it nobly? This is also an abiding theme in Japanese poetry and reflection, especially in the most ancient fragments. Our temporality and its abrupt end—for we are all mortal—is of the greatest concern to all of us, perhaps especially to me because I am now fairly old. Also, however, it is of interest because the Christian understanding of death has had to adjust fairly radically its view of how death came about and so how death may be related to God the creator.

Our tradition has generally followed St. Paul and some of the implications of Genesis by ascribing death to sin, the sin of Adam—"as in Adam all die." However, with the new scientific and historical understanding of the cosmic, the evolutionary, and the human past, this explanation of death—that it came in recent times as a result of the sin of the first human pair—is no longer possible for us who live within, and so accept, a scientific, technological culture. We know, if we know anything at all, that the cycle of life and death is as old as is organic life itself, and that that life stretches back several billions of years—long before anything resembling the human appeared on earth. If God has created all life and if creation is good—two very fundamental Christian beliefs—then death, as the universal terminus of all life, is a part of God's good creation and must be understood accordingly. And so our question is: how are we to do this?

The problem is that death appears to all of us as the contrary, the sharp opposite, of all that is of value, of all that is good—for value depends on life and seems to stop with the end of life. How, therefore, could death, which seems the exact opposite of life, be part of a good creation? For this reason many religions, including much of Christianity, have solved the problem of death by reducing the value of life; life and death together form a vast wheel of suffering, a "vale of tears"—and so salvation is to transcend or escape from *both* life and death. This is profound, but it denies the goodness of creation and the potential value of life here on earth. Most modern religion, certainly most modern Christianity, has rejected such a transcendental or supernatural resolution.

This problem is by no means an easy one, for death is a final and ultimate shock to the values of our life and that of those we love. But if we reflect on it carefully and try to see all sides of the intricate relation of life to death, we may find a clue to understanding, in a new way, how death can be a part of God's good creation. Certainly, for modern biological science, there can be no life—once life reaches a certain stage—without also death. In each species, new life is possible only because old life dies. Mutations and changes of species are possible because of the death of older forms. Any territory would be overrun if all life lived on. As I reminded my students, there would be no room for them in any college classroom if all the old grads were still there! New life in nature arises out of the death of the old. All early religious myths make this point, and this was certainly the experience by early humans of the nature around them. Seeds died in the ground in order that they might rise again to life; spring could come only after the seeming death of winter had covered over everything living; and sun and moon, the

king and the queen of life, each in its own way descends into
the realm of death in order to reappear with new life in its ap-
pointed time. In nature, death is a necessary part of life, an
apparent condition of it. And in all early religions, the gods of
life were also the rulers of the realm of the dead.

This pattern in nature, that there is new life only where
there is participation in death as well, is surprisingly dupli-
cated, or reappears, in the spiritual existence of human beings.
Neoorthodox theology drew a sharp distinction between the
realm of nature and the personal realm of spirit. We, however,
no longer do this, and especially on this point, for it is impossible to become fully human unless one is willing to face the
prospect of death. No person or value can be defended unless
one is ready to suffer and if necessary to die for that person or
value—whether we speak of one's family or the integrity of another person or of freedom and justice in the community. None
of these values of life can be effectively furthered without
courage, the readiness to risk oneself for that in which one believes or for those to whom one is loyal—and this means facing
the prospect of death. Hence courage is the basis of any virtue,
the courage to stand where we must stand. In this sense, there
is no real life unless it confronts and absorbs, takes in and
makes a part of itself, death. As in nature, so in human existence life arises out of the prospect of death—no culture has
known this as well as has Japan.

For this reason the biblical God is the Lord of life but
also the Lord over death; God is the giver of both to God's mortal creatures. Life and death in God's world are thus not completely antithetical, and the value of life depends in part on the
presence of death in the good creation—and on our faith and
our courage in facing the certainty of death. Finally, therefore,
we can be content and can believe in the message that as God
has given to us all both life and death, so in the end the divine
Power and Mercy will give us eternal life when we have come to
the end of our allotted time.

index

absoluteness
  particularity, universality and, 130–31
  plurality and relative, 134–41
  sacrificing of, 145
academics
  disunity of, 88
  freedom of, 23–24
Act 590
  basis of, 21–22
  problems with, 22–24
agape, 123, 141
altruism, 78
American Civil Liberties Union, 21, 22, 29, 57
American theology
  ecology, nature and, 113–16
  evolutionary thought of, 114
  fundamentalist revival and, 116–18
  relativity and symbolism of, 114
  religious pluralism for, 110–13
  since Niebuhr and Tillich, 109–10
  union of science, philosophy of science and, 115
anxiety, 53–54
  being, nonbeing and, 92–93, 102–4
  courage over, 93
  creature, spirit and, 82–83, 91
  emptiness of religious cause for, 91, 102
  of finitude, 92–93, 96–97
  meaningless as root of, 149
  moral, 102–3
  space/time basis of, 95–97, 154
atheism, 57
atonement, 101
authoritarianism, 150, 160–61
autonomy
  dangers of, 93–94, 117–18
  profanized, 148
  unraveling of, 148–49, 151–52

barbarism, 4
Barth, Karl, 3, 69, 76, 99–100
being
  finite, 92
  nonbeing and, 89, 92–94, 102, 103–4, 140
  religion understood through, 89
  self-awareness necessary for, 89–89
Being-Itself, 103
  as non-Christian, 104
  spirit, God and, 105
belief, 35
betrayal, 165
Beyond Tragedy (Niebuhr), 80
biblical faith (view), 80, 82, 86, 119
Buddhism, 47, 103, 109, 136–37, 153
  desire and, 68, 113, 153
  higher consciousness of, 112
  inclusive revelation in, 129–30
  no soul doctrine of, 141
  parity, particularity and, 127–28
  true symbols of, 112–13

capitalism, 153–54
categories, 94–95
causality
  first, second, 27
  space, time and, 64–66, 95
Christian America, 133
Christian Coalition, 117
  political aspirations of, 43, 57
  reinterpreting Church and State by, 58
Christianity. *See also* Genesis
  absoluteness of, 50, 124
  Being-Itself as non, 104
  finality of revelation of, 129, 131
  First Amendment, creationism and, 22–23
  God's religion in, 45

heresy of two gods for, 30
identity emphasized in, 141
liberal, 51
nation of, 47
non-Christians accusing of, 126
nonfundamentalist form of, 46
superiority to parity for, 111–12, 121–26
true symbols of, 112–13
Western culture as basis in, 63–64
Christianity and Society, 75
church(es)
  challenge of evils by, 79
  current perspective of Genesis by, 58–59
  intrinsic unity with sacramental presence
    in, 106–7
  science supported by, 33, 57
  separation of State and, 58
class, power of, 77, 150–51
community
  history of, 158
  morality, individuality and, 77–78, 84
concern, ultimate, 46, 91, 92, 118, 149
  elusiveness of, 153
concupiscence, 113, 146–48, 153
confession, 84
consciousness
  cosmos and, 148
  higher, 112, 129
  modern historical, 162
  religious, 111–12
conservatives, 54
corporation(s), 7–8
cosmology, 65–66
  genetics and, 114
courage, 93–94, 97, 115
  of Americans, 152–53
  with mortality, 171
Courage to Be, The (Tillich), 87
creation
  changing perspective (as witness) and, 61
  cosmology of, 65–66
  creationists and, 56–58
  divine intervention of, 56
  the fall and, 100
  God, humans and, 67–71
  as good, 66, 169–70
  historical perspective of, 58–59
  humans as likeness of God in, 64
  male dominance in, 68
  message of Genesis for, 62–67
  religious faith, science and, 55
  religious viewpoint of, 31
  rethinking of the Mosaic account of,
    58–62
  time, space and, 64–66

creation science
  denial of scientific subjects with, 43,
    52–53, 56
  evolution vs., 21–22, 31–32
  false portrayal as science by, 23
  literal reading of Genesis by, 48
  scientific naturalism vs., 37
  validity of, 56–57
creationism, x
  defense against, 29–32
  naturalistic explanation vs. God and,
    25–26
  origins "scientifically" explained by,
    24–25
  as particular form of religion, 30
  supernatural unrepeatable aspect of, 27
creationists
  as Christian fundamentalist, 56
  opposition to science based on atheism
    by, 57
  scientists as leader of, 33, 56–57
  scripture as literally true for, 56
  theologians and, 33
  trial of, 21
  ultimate origins question unanswered by,
    27
  use of technology by, 58, 117
creativity
  basis of, 82, 141
  courage necessity of, 93
  of groups, 158–59
  history influenced by, 80
Creator, 30
creature
  creatureliness of, 81–82
  spirit and, 14–16, 19, 81–82
critical realism, 147
culture, 101
  autonomous, 110
  creative, 90–91
  development of modern, 94
  disunity of, 88–89
  fundamentalism above, 52
  Genesis as tradition of, 55, 64
  Hebraic culture as basis of Western,
    63–64
  Hellenic culture as basis of Western, 64
  myth and, 11, 91
  myth, creativity, sin and, 17–18
  myth devoid in modern, 13
  reason and religion ambiguous to, 79
  religion, technology, part of modern,
    33–34
  Religious Right and modern, 53–54
  religious substance of, 91, 107

science as center of, 38
theonomous, 107
universality and particularity of, 128–29

Darwin, Charles, 35, 56
desire, 5, 68, 113, 147, 153
destiny, 64–65, 93, 144, 158
Dewey, John, 79, 135, 160–61
dialectic
    God's actions as, 165
    of infinity and finite, 137–39, 140–41,
        145
    material, 14
discrimination, 8, 47, 49–50, 77, 84, 117
dissenters, non-Christian, 45
dualism, 19, 88

ecology, 147
    American theology, nature and, 113–16
ecumenical movement, 122, 131–32
End of an Era (Niebuhr), 76
Enlightenment, 94
epistemology, 147–48
eschatology, Christian/Hebrew, 13
estrangement, 146
evil, 17
    churches challenge of, 79
    cosmic, 26
    good before, 63
    possibilities for, 67
evolution
    creation science vs., 21–22, 31–32
    God and, 35

faith, 18, 61–62
    biblical, 80, 82, 85
    as growing morality of society, 76
    requirements of, 122–23
    universal religious basis of, 112
fall, the, 63, 66–67, 85, 104
    creation and, 100
fanaticism, 40, 48, 91, 116–17, 132
Fascism, German, 48–49
finite, the
    infinity and, 137–39, 140–41, 145
First Amendment, 47
    Christian primacy and, 22–23
    contravening of, 30, 31
    religion limitations in, 48, 50, 57–58
forgiveness, 101
freedom
    admittance of sin for, 84–85
    government, groups and, 158–59
    history, sin and, 85–86
    human, 163, 167–68

fundamentalism, 47
    absolute truth of, 44
    American theology and revival of, 116–18
    creationism and, 25
    discrimination by, 8, 47, 49–50
    growth of, 33, 39
    heteronomous, 94
    historical, 30, 44
    modernity denounced by, 51–52
    as reaction to liberal Protestantism, 37
    replacing of science by, 17
    science, authoritarianism and, 48–49, 53
    tolerance of, 133

gender, 68, 81, 84, 151, 152
Genesis, 23, 24, 30, 34
    cosmology (scientific) and, 65–66
    creation as good in, 66
    historical perspective of, 58–59
    literal interpretation of, 48, 56
    message of, 62–67
    pollution and, 69
    as pre-scientific myth, 36
    relevance of, 55
    religious, not literal, meanings of,
        61–62
    science, geology influence on, 59–60
    as source of alternative science, 36
    time/space and, 64–66
    as tradition for cultural life, 55
    as truths of revelation, 62
Germany, 94, 151
Gish, Duane, 49
God
    absoluteness of, 50, 60, 64, 85, 103
    analogies of, 9
    as Being-Itself, 102–4
    creation, humans and, 63, 67–71
    creation "out of nothing" by, 31
    as Creator, 30, 60, 63, 127, 167
    death and eternal life through, 171
    dialectical actions of, 165
    (divine) acts through causes by, 163, 164,
        167–68
    doctrine of, 7
    freedom, humans, future and, 163,
        167–68
    goodness, care and mercy of, 63, 66,
        85–86, 171
    grace of, 85–86
    humans in image of, 8, 10, 64, 71, 80, 85
    humans, nature and, 3
    is dead, 110
    as Living, 116
    nature and image of, 8–10, 71, 116

nonbeing and mystery that transcends, 141

open question of, 28

personal character of, 4

pride defying of, 83

revealed elsewhere, 124

science and presence of, 28

Scripture as witness of presence and activity of, 61–62

as source of being, 103

spirit and personal, 105–7

status of, 102–4

will of, 46

the word and, 10

good, 63, 66–67, 170

gospel, the, 45

government, 8

    groups, freedom and, 158–59

    impinging of academic freedom by, 23–24

grace, 85–86, 124

    other religion's, 129

    others and our, 137

greed, 68, 71

groundedness, 7, 112

groups

    government, freedom and, 158–59

    self-interest of, 78

health, 102

heteronomy, 91, 93, 103, 118

    radical, 148–54

Hinduism, 47, 128

    inclusive revelation in, 129–30

history, 101

    changing nature of, 61, 162–63

    creativity influence on, 80

    events and understanding of, 164–68

    freedom, humans and, 163

    freedom, sin and, 85–86

    groups, freedom, government and, 157–59

    Hellenistic viewpoint of, 162

    modern consciousness and, 162

    no universal reason in, 163

    as progressive, 4, 76, 113, 145, 164

    scientific, democratic development of civilization for, 13

    sin, judgment and, 161, 166

    social symbols and, 160

    theology and, 162–64, xii

human(s)

    beginning subordination/precariousness of, 70

    creativity of, 80, 82

    creature and spirit aspects of, 15–16, 19

    creatureliness of, 81

dependency on nature by, 5

free will of, 64–65

freedom, future, God and, 163, 167–68

God, creation and, 67–71

as image of God, 8, 10, 64, 71, 80, 85

myth, evil and hope in, 11

myth as self-understanding, 14, 17–19

nature, God and, 4, 10

nature's domination by, 68, 70–71

need for space by, 96, 155

personal character of, 4

recognition of universality of, 8

self-reflection for, 40

spirit as seat of, 105–6

I-it, 4

I-thou, 4, 104

ideology

    fundamentalism, authoritarianism and, 48–49, 53

    idolatry vs., 46

imago dei, 68, 80

indeterminism, 6

infinity

    and finite, 137–39, 140–41, 145

intelligence, informed, 79

Islam, 47

Jesus Christ, 86

    New Being through, 106

    sacrificing of absoluteness of, 145

Judaism, 29, 61, 122

    absoluteness of God in, 50

    persecution of, 87, 100

    space, terror and, 155

    Western culture as basis in, 63–64

Judaism. See also Genesis

justice, 50, 136

    vs. sacramental demonry, 151

    workers for, 77

kairos, 144, 156

Keiji, Nishitani, 5

language

    mythical, 17–18

    mythical, philosophical, and scientific, 12

liberals, 75–76, 122–23

Little Rock, Arkansas, 21, 57

logos, 90, 138, 144

love

    absolute, 141

    of other, 122, 124

male dominance, 68, 81

meaning, ultimate, 149

metaphysical, 128

modernity, 94, 162
  dissolving of religious/moral principles in,
    117
  fundamentalism denunciation of, 51–52
  myth, science and, 12–13
Moral Man and Immoral Society (Niebuhr),
    76
morality, 7, 169–71
  action for, 83, 135
  America's amoral mass and, 149–50
  anxiety with, 101–2
  Christian, 8
  individual vs. community, 77–78, 84
  organic, not sin, 169–70
  religious consciousness, the individual
    and, 111
  religious sense of ultimacy and grounding
    of, 118
  resolution of, 7
  self becomes through, 105–6
  spirit of, 16
  unraveling of, 117, 151
mortality, 16
  as good, not sin, 81
  meaningless and, 102
  supernatural resolution rejected for, 170
mystery, infinite, 138, 140–41
mysticism, 36, 111–12, 129–30
myth
  changing role of, 12–14
  culture, creativity, sin and, 17–18
  democracy vs. communism, 39
  of the fall, 85, 104
  fundamental value of, 11, 63, 91
  higher civilization as, 14
  inner and outer value of, 12
  modern culture devoid of, 13
  science, objectivity and, 12–13
  of science vs. religion, 12–13, 33, 38–39
  speech of, 17–18
  time and, 65

National Association of Biology Teachers,
    29, 34
National Council of Churches, 33
naturalism, scientific, 36–37
nature, xi
  American theology, ecology and,
    113–16
  as anthropological backdrop, 3, 69
  as cause and effects, 4
  human civilization dependent on, 5
  human domination of, 68, 70–71
  as image of God, 8–10, 71, 115–16
  mystic, 146
  preservation of, 114
  science, greed, and crisis of, 4–6

theology response to crisis of, 7–10
  the word and, 10
Nature and Destiny of Man, The (Niebuhr),
    80
Nazis, 87, 132–33
neoorthodox, 99–101
  acceptance of science's nature by, 101,
    109–10
  doctrinal faith over love for, 123
  fear of dogmatism (but not in modern
    age) by, 117
New Being, 106, 145
New Testament, 67
Niebuhr, Reinhold, 16, 100, 109
  ethics, politics, social affairs and, 75–76
  history's meaning for, 85–86
  the human spirit and, 80–85
  Judaism and, 164
  political activism of, 75–76
  realism and optimism of, 76–80
Old Testament, 164–65
ontology, 87–90, 92, 144
  being, anxiety and, 101–2
  God's status and, 102–4
  space/time and, 100
  theology influenced by, 101–4
order, 77
origin(s)
  nonprovability of, 25
  scientific vs. religious account for, 32
  ultimate, 27
Other, personal, 105

pantheism, 129
parity
  rough, xi, 121–22, 131, 143
  from superiority to, 121–26
particularity
  pluralism, universality and, 126–32, 138
patriotism, 78
piety, personal, 111
pluralism, xi, 3
  complexity and ambiguity of, 132–34
  particularity, universality and, 126–32,
    138
  relative absoluteness and, 134–41
  religious, 110–13, 143–45
  superiority to parity for, 121–26
politics. *See also* Religious Right
  religion with, 43–44
  theocracy as, 46–47
postmodernism, 11, 110, 153, 162
power
  class, 77
  dominance of, 77–78, 153–54, 165
praxis, 135–37, 140, 141
  pride, ultimacy, 83

privatissimum, 100
prophetic principle, 46, 50–51
Protestantism, liberal, 37
psalms, 9

reason
    controlling, 90, 148
    as culture creative power, 90
    informed, 79
    logos and, 90
    no universal, 163
    technical, 90
relative absoluteness. *See* absoluteness
relativism
    historical, 110
    self-understanding of science and, 114
religion, American, 121
    nature and, 145–48
    radical heteronomy and, 148–54
    religious pluralism and, 143–45
    space and, 154–56
religion(s). *See also* pluralism
    atheistic humanism, 22, 24
    being as basis of, 89
    confidence, courage through, 45
    corruption of state through establishment
        of, 50
    demonic possibilities of, 132–133
    destructive ways of, 40–41
    establishment of, 47–50
    faith and, 112
    intolerable, 132
    judgment from beyond essential for, 18
    liberal, nondogmatic, 79
    monotheistic, 30–31
    mystical core of, 130–31
    myth as language of, 11
    not as universal, 128, 144
    persistence of, 39–40
    politics with, 44
    as prescience, 35
    regionalism of, 47
    relativity of, 123–24
    relativizing and pointing beyond, 113,
        131, 136, 141
    responsibility of, 35
    science conflict with, 29, 53–54
    self-limiting, societal limiting of, 48
    technology, science effects increase
        growth of, 39
    transcendent relationship to, 46
    as ultimate concern, 89, 92
    universal experience of nature of, 9
religious horizon, 158, 161
Religious Right, 43–54. *See also* Christian
        Coalition
    absolute religious truth of, 45–47

    denial of rational reflection in social mat-
        ters by, 44
    denial of scientific subjects by religious
        truths of, 43
    denunciation of modernity by, 51–52
    elements of truth in other traditions and,
        50–53
    establishment of religion and, 47–50
    political power of, 43, 49, 54, 57, 132–33
    radical heteronomy of, 148
    radical individualistic capitalism of, 154
    Republican Party influenced by, 49, 54,
        57
    responses of modern culture to, 53–54
Religious Socialist movement, 87
Republican Party, 49, 54, 57
revelation
    Christian, 123, 139
    event of, 112
    finality of Christian, 129, 131
    inclusiveness of, 129–130
    objectivity of, 110
    symbols of, 127
    understanding others, 141
    universal, 106

sacramental consecrations, 150–151
salvation, 102, 170
Schleiermacher, Friedrich, 60–61, 85, 124,
        129
science
    as cause and effect, 4, 7, 15
    confusion about, 26–27
    creation science vs., 21–22, 31–32, 43,
        52–53
    defense for, 29–32
    destructive ways of, 40–41
    as dissolving of religious truth, 35–36
    fear of, 3
    fundamentalism, authoritarianism and,
        48–49, 53
    as hermeneutical search, 6
    limits of, 28
    military marriage with, 79
    myth, objectivity and, 12–13
    natural theology interconnection with,
        6–7
    nature, greed and, 5–6
    neoorthodox acceptance of, 101, 109–10,
        114
    new philosophy of, 6
    nonbeneficial nature of, 39–40
    objective and subjective for, 89
    philosophy of science, theology and, 37,
        115
    religions conflict with, 29, 53–54
    responsibility of, 35

Scriptures as root of, 65–66
spiritual basis of, 15–16
truth as aim of, 15, 27
theories and methods for, 26–28, 37
warning value of, 7
science, creation. *See* creation science; creationism
Scripture
   Genesis, 23, 31
   God of, 9
   human aspects of, 62
   as literally true, 56
   opening of, 55
   science's roots in, 65–66
   spectacles of, 10
   as witness of presence and activity of God, 61–62
self-awareness, 92, 147
self-centeredness, 82–83
self-concern, 18, 77, 85
self-criticism, 48, 107, 118
self-deception, 84–85
self-interest, 77–78, 84, 165–66
self-sacrifice, 78, 145
self-transcendence. *See* transcendence
Shaking of the Foundations, The (Tillich), 87
Shinto, 116, 132
sin, 5–6
   anxiety basis of, 97
   communal, 84
   consciousness of, 101
   consequence of, 55
   culture, creativity, myth and, 17–18
   estrangement as, 93, 146–47
   forgiveness of, 101
   history, freedom and, 85–86
   history, judgment and, 161
   hypocrisy and, 16
   mortality not as, 81
   nature's destruction and, 114
   nature's domination as, 71
   original, 85
   self-transcendence, creatureliness and, 82
   ultimate, 83
   universality of, 77, 80, 85–86, 166
   wealthy groups source of, 7
society
   dilemmas of technological, 33
   limiting of religion by, 48
   objectivity difficult in, 79
   participation in progressive process of, 152–53
   technology, science and, 23
space
   border and defense of, 96

causality, substance, time, and, 94–95
linear nature of, 64–66
ontology and, 100
religious situation and, 154–56
spirit
   creature and, 14–16, 19
   health of, 102
   the human, 80–85
   personal relation with God through, 105–7
   science and, 15–16
   self-transcending, 16
   universality but finite origin of, 81–82
St. Augustine, 63, 64, 81
superiority
   collapsing of, 125–26
   faith and Christian, 123–24
   Western dominance for, 125
symbol(s), 9
   Christian, 23, 140
   credible system of, 39
   essential value of, 17–18
   gestalt of, 127
   of image of God, 62, 85
   nonoffense of others, 127
   of original sin, 85
   relative manifestation of absolute meaning in, 140
   social, 160
   systems of, 32
   true, 112–13, 145
   understanding through, 85
Systematic Theology (Tillich), 105, 147

temporality, 115
theism, 112, 127
theocracy, 46–47, 49, 118, 133–34
theologians
   biblical, 99–101
   christomorphic, 104–7
   creationists and, 33
   current perspective of Genesis by, 58–59
   dialectical, 99, 109
   historical/cultural influence on, 101
theology. *See also* American theology; religion(s)
   constructive, xi
   evolutionary thought in, 114
   God through nature's glory for, 10
   history and, –5, 162–64
   I-thou of, 4
   of liberation, 152
   limits of, 60–61
   male dominance in, 68, 81
   natural, 6–7, 27, 106
   nature's crisis and response of, 7–10
   nonfundamentalist, 101

ontology aspect of, 101–4
science interconnection with natural, 6–7
theonomy, 93–94, 103, 107
    meaning of, 148–49, 152
Tillich, Paul, 46, 54, 109, 129
    art, psychotherapy, philosophy and, 75
    background of, 87–88
    being and nonbeing for, 92–94
    biblical theologians and, 99–101
    christomorphic theologians and, 104–7
    nature and, 145–48
    the neoorthodox and, 99–101
    ontological issues for, 101–4
    ontological philosophy and personal exis-
        tentially of, 87–89
    radical heteronomy and, 148–54
    religion and culture for, 90–91
    religious pluralism and, 143–45
    space and, 94–96, 100, 154–56
    time and space for, 94–97
time
    anxiety's basis in, 95–96
    causality, substance, space and, 94–95
    grounds of religious existence in space
        and, 95–97
    linear nature of, 64–66
    ontology and, 100
tolerance
    of diversity, 48
    ecumenical, 132
    Religious Right and, 133
transcendence, 16, 46, 83, 139
    confession and self, 84
    self, 80–81
    sin, creatureliness and, 82
truth
    absolute, 44–47
    creaturely, 83

other religion's, 124, 129
others and our, 137
    religious, 43, 60
    revelation and, 62
    science's aim in, 15, 27, 38
    scientific vs. religious, 36–37, 59–60
    scientist's integration and reflection on,
        38
    seeking for, 83
    true but not literal, 85
tyranny, 132–34, 151

ultimacy, horizon of, 158, 161, 166–67
Ultimate Being, 19
ultimate concern. See concern, ultimate
uncertainty principle, 6
universality
    pluralism, particularity and, 126–32, 138
    self-sacrificing of, 145
University of Chicago, Divinity School of,
        38

values
    concern for, 91
    family, 51
    ground for, 136
    objectivity separate from, 18–19
    self-deception of, 84
Vedanta, 111

war, self-interest of, 84
World Council of Churches, 33

Zen, 111